MAJOR INDUSTRIAL RESEARCH UNIT STUDIES

No. 65

EMPLOYEE RELATIONS TRENDS AND PRACTICES IN THE TEXTILE INDUSTRY

by

RICHARD L. ROWAN

and

ROBERT E. BARR

INDUSTRIAL RESEARCH UNIT

The Wharton School

University of Pennsylvania

Philadelphia, Pennsylvania 19104-6358

Foreword

This study is the fourth contribution to the work in the Wharton Industrial Research Unit pertaining to labor and personnel policies and practices in various industries in which unions are either losing ground or have failed to become a serious factor. Previous studies include *Collective Bargaining and the Decline of the United Mine Workers* (1984), *Open Shop Construction Revisited* (1984), and *Deregulation and the Decline of the Unionized Trucking Industry* (1986). It also marks a continuation of my interest in the textile industry which began in the 1960s with the publication of *The Negro in the Textile Industry* (1970) and continued in the 1970s with a publication pertaining to employment problems associated with the Occupational Safety and Health Act, *The Impact of OSHA: A Study of the Effects of the Occupational Safety and Health Act on Three Key Industries—Aerospace, Chemicals, and Textiles* (1978). The co-author, Robert E. Barr, received his bachelor's degree from the University of South Carolina and worked for several years in the textile industry before obtaining a Master of Business Administration Degree at the Wharton School. He is now with a high technology firm in Massachusetts. During the early part of the study, I was assisted by Christine Jadach Rodriguez, an undergraduate student in the Wharton School, who has since finished her law degree at Harvard University and is now employed by a major consulting firm in Boston. The project could not have been undertaken without support from the Labor Relations Council of the Wharton School.

In addition to the customary research activities, including a search of the literature, I have spent many hours in textile plants in the South where most of the industry is concentrated at the present time. Executives of numerous companies gave freely of their time and allowed me to explore their facilities and activities. The study would have been impossible without their cooperation. The cooperation of textile executives was supplemented by assistance from the American Textile Manufacturers Institute for which I am most grateful. I also appreciate the assistance of several trade union officials who made materials available.

All field work was done by me; however, both authors wish to thank our librarian, Mrs. Sue Torelli, our secretarial staff including Miss Rita Gorman, and our editor, Mrs. Kathryn Pearcy, for their assistance. Mrs. Marthenia Perrin, Business Administrator of the Industrial Research Unit, handled the administrative details associated with this and all of the Unit's other activities. As in all works published by the Wharton Industrial Research Unit, the senior author is solely responsible for the research and for all opinions expressed, none of which should be attributed to the University of Pennsylvania.

Richard L. Rowan, *Co-Director*
Industrial Research Unit
University of Pennsylvania

Philadelphia
July 1986

TABLE OF CONTENTS

LIST OF TABLES

TABLE   PAGE

CHAPTER I

CHAPTER II

Introduction

The textile industry is a leading employer in the United States. Although employment has been declining over the past decade, approximately 700,000 people remain employed in the industry in 1986. The percentage of production workers in textile plants is probably higher than that found in any other industry, and the majority of these employees are classified as unskilled laborers or semi-skilled operatives. Today, the industry is heavily concentrated in the three southern states of North Carolina, South Carolina, and Georgia and, within those states, textile operations are further concentrated in a total of ten counties. The major concern of this study is to examine employment trends and industrial relations/personnel policy and practices in the textile industry. Industrial development in the South, technological changes, economic dislocations caused by increasing imports, and a shifting composition of the labor force have confronted personnel managers with challenging problems. Between 1981 and 1985 an intensive survey of employment trends, practices, and problems was made and the results are analyzed in this study.

RESEARCH METHODOLOGY

This study relies on the techniques of survey, questionnaire, and personal interviews in the field. A careful selection of companies in North Carolina, South Carolina, and Georgia, representative of the industry, was made for follow-up study.

Definition of the Industry

For purposes of this study, the textile industry is defined as closely as possible in terms of the Standard Industrial Classification (SIC 22) system. The SIC 22 group, Textile Mill Products, is defined as follows:

> This major group includes establishments engaged in performing any of the following operations: (1) preparation of fiber and subsequent manufacturing of yarn, thread, braids, twine, and cordage; (2) man-

ufacturing broad woven fabric, narrow woven fabric, knit fabric, and carpets and rugs from yarn; (3) dyeing and finishing fiber, yarn, and knit apparel; (4) coating, waterproofing, or otherwise treating fabric; (5) the integrated manufacture of knit apparel and other finished articles from yarn; and (6) the manufacture of felt goods, lace goods, bonded-fiber fabrics, and miscellaneous textiles.[1]

Some of the major classifications in the industry include those shown in Table I-1.

TABLE I-1

Textile Mill Products (SIC Code 22)
Major Standard Industrial Classifications

221	Broad Woven Fabric Mills, Cotton
222	Broad Woven Fabric Mills, Man-Made Fiber and Silk
223	Broad Woven Fabric Mills, Wool
224	Narrow Fabrics and Other Smallwares Mills: Cotton, Wool, Silk and Man-Made Fiber
225	Knitting Mills
226	Dyeing and Finishing Textiles, except Wool Fabrics and Knit Goods
227	Floor Covering Mills
228	Yarn and Thread Mills
229	Miscellaneous Textile Goods

Source: U.S. Bureau of the Budget, *Standard Industrial Classification Manual*, 1967, pp. 54–64.

Employment in SIC 22 was volatile over the period 1939 to 1968, but the general trend was downward. Between 1939 and 1956, employment ranged between 1.0 and 1.3 million with a peak reached in 1942, when 1,342,000 people were employed. In 1957, textile employment dropped below 1.0 million and has not exceeded that figure since.[2] By 1984, employment had dropped to 755,000 and in January 1986 the figure stood at 699,000.[3]

The Questionnaire

The questionnaire distributed to the participants in this study is shown in the Appendix. Questions were designed to solicit quantitative information, as well as subjective, qualitative responses, in regard to the whole range of employment policies and practices. Respondents were free to answer as they felt appropriate, and this helped to identify variances between policy and practice. The data collected permitted comparison among different firms on issues such

[1] U.S. Bureau of the Budget, *Standard Industrial Classification Manual*, 1967, pp. 54–64.
[2] Richard L. Rowan, *The Negro in the Textile Industry* (Philadelphia: Industrial Research Unit, The Wharton School, University of Pennsylvania, 1970), pp. 2–3.
[3] *Textile World*, Vol. 136, No. 1 (January 1986), p. 18.

TABLE I-2

The Textile Industry
Survey Responses by State and County

North Carolina	38	South Carolina	41	Georgia	7
Gaston	8	Greenville	17	Whitfield	4
Guilford	7	Spartanburg	8	Troup	1
Rockingham	6	Anderson	7	Floyd	1
Alamance	4	Lancaster	2	Muscogee	1
Catawba	4	York	2		
Cabarrus	2	Chester	1		
Randolph	2	Laurens	1		
Cleveland	1	Newberry	1		
Johnston	1	Oconee	1		
Pitt	1	Pickens	1		
Rutherford	1				
Stanly	1				

as wages, benefits, and work scheduling. Follow-up interviews with companies were greatly enhanced by the availability of information gathered in the survey process.

Locations and Companies Selected for Study

The questionnaire was completed by 86 responding units representing 28 companies in 26 counties within North Carolina, South Carolina, and Georgia. States, counties, and companies were selected because of their large textile employment base and, in some cases, on the advice of industry leaders. A unique feature of this study is that it reflects employment activity in those areas of the country where a majority of the textile industry is concentrated. Table I-2 shows the number of questionnaires completed by state and county. The top seven counties surveyed were: Greenville, SC (17); Gaston, NC (8); Spartanburg, SC (8); Anderson, SC (7); Rockingham, NC (6); Guilford, NC (7); and Whitfield, GA (4). Figure I-1 shows a map of the textile study area.

Interviews were conducted at the corporate and plant levels with participation by representatives of 24 companies. Eight of the ten largest textile mill companies, as shown in Table I-3, were included for intensive study. Senior managers in the personnel function, as well as staff and operating management, were interviewed. Further insights were gained by interviews with labor law firms, trade groups, government officials, and union representatives in the textile industry.

FIGURE I-1

Textile Study Area

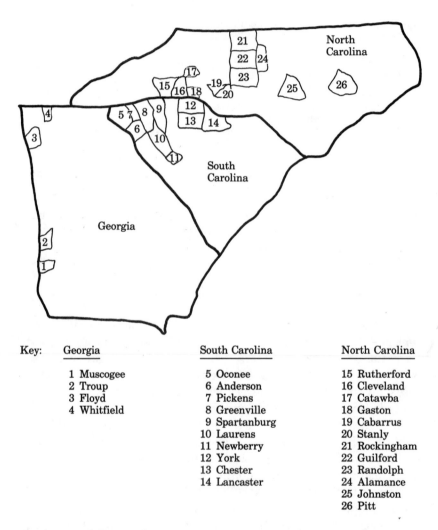

Key:

Georgia	South Carolina	North Carolina
1 Muscogee	5 Oconee	15 Rutherford
2 Troup	6 Anderson	16 Cleveland
3 Floyd	7 Pickens	17 Catawba
4 Whitfield	8 Greenville	18 Gaston
	9 Spartanburg	19 Cabarrus
	10 Laurens	20 Stanly
	11 Newberry	21 Rockingham
	12 York	22 Guilford
	13 Chester	23 Randolph
	14 Lancaster	24 Alamance
		25 Johnston
		26 Pitt

Background Research

Historical data are important in understanding the present employment situation in the textile industry. These data are presented and analyzed in Chapters II, III, and IV. All background data have been presented using regional definitions established by the U.S. Bureau of Census (Table I-4). When data from other government agencies did not conform with the Census Bureau definition it was

TABLE I-3

The Ten Largest[1] (Sales) Textile Mill Companies, 1985

Company	Headquarters	Sales ($000)	Assets ($000)	Net Income ($000)	Employees
Burlington Industries	Greensboro, NC	3,168,760	2,294,402	62,399	53,000
J.P. Stevens	New York, NY	2,144,183	1,172,578	21,969	32,700
Armstrong World Ind.	Lancaster, PA	1,569,181	951,129	92,230	19,992
West Point-Pepperell	West Point, GA	1,333,246	760,865	55,725	22,100
Spring Industries	Fort Mill, SC	944,990	614,989	36,071	16,800
Collins & Aikman	New York, NY	930,535	475,763	48,054	10,400
M. Lowenstein	New York, NY	639,580	381,952	30,636	9,300
Fieldcrest Mills	Eden, NC	572,921	363,427	4,143	10,961
United Merchant & Manufacturers	New York, NY	563,193	430,661	12,350	9,000
Riegel Textile	Greenville, SC	435,185	253,957	(16,088)	7,400

Source: *Fortune,* April 29, 1985, pp. 265–286.

[1] These are the only Textile Mill Companies (SIC 22) found in the Fortune 500. The recent merger movement in the textile industry will be reflected in 1986 figures. Fieldcrest has purchased Cannon Mills, Springs has purchased M. Lowenstein; West Point-Pepperell purchased Cluet, Peabody; and J.P. Stevens has entered into an agreement to purchase Burlington's Sheet and Towel division.

TABLE I-4

Regions as Defined by the U.S. Bureau of Census

Northeast—CT, ME, MA, NH, NJ, NY, PA, RI, VT

North Central—IL, IN, IA, KS, MI, MN, MD, NB, OH, WI

South—AL, AR, DE, DC, FL, GA, KY, LA, MD, MS, OK, NC, SC, TN, TX, VA, WV

West—AK, AZ, CA, CO, HA, ID, MT, NM, NV, ND, OR, SD, UT, WA, WY

Source: Bureau of the Census, U.S. Department of Commerce, *1970 Census of Population, Detailed Characteristics, U.S. Summary,* Vol. PC(1)-D1, p. 1–587.

recompiled into the regions shown in Table I-4 in order to ensure consistency in comparing data throughout the study.

CHAPTER II

The Structure of the
Textile Industry

Industrial structure is important in determining the conditions under which industrial relations and personnel policies and practices will be developed. An understanding of the industrial environment in which a company or companies operate facilitates an analysis of employment problems. A more realistic appraisal of the management of human resources, both past and present, can be made through a thorough knowledge of an industry's structure. The purpose of this chapter is to discuss the general background of the textile industry with particular reference to production processes, industrial characteristics, and manpower.

TECHNOLOGY AND THE PRODUCTION PROCESSES

Although the textile industry is one of the oldest in the country, it has only recently begun to modernize in response to competitive pressures resulting from rising imports, increasing producer prices, and a shrinking labor force.

Textile production is labor intensive and employs a majority of unskilled workers and semi-skilled operatives.[1] This emphasis on minimal skills results from task design within the production process. Textile tasks are typically simple and discrete with one task feeding another (see Textile Product Workflow, Figure II-1). Horizontal integration is usually avoided which maximizes the pool of potential employees and minimizes the impact of labor turnover and associated training and productivity costs.

The production process begins when cotton bales, shipped from ginning plants, are opened and fed into blending machines. These

---

[1] The Textile Industry is essentially decentralized. In 1977, there were 7,202 firms with 4,131 of these employing less than 20 individuals. This domination of the small firm is reinforced, when one considers that the top 15 publicly held firms employed over 26 percent of the industry total themselves, with the remainder employed by 7,187 firms. See U.S, Bureau of the Census, *1977 Census of Manufacturers* and "How the Top 15 Publicly Held U.S. Textile Companies Fared in Operations in Fiscal 1977," *Textile World*, Vol. 128, No. 7, July 1978.

FIGURE II-1

Textile Production Workflow

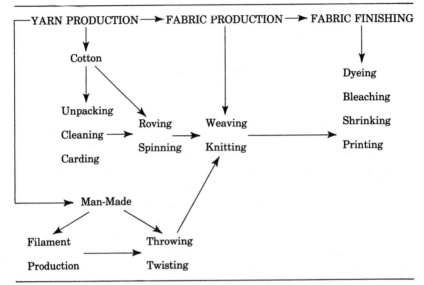

Source: Council on Wage and Price Stability, Staff Report, *A Study of the Textile and Apparel Industries,* 1978, p. 9.

blenders provide an initial loosening, cleaning, and mixing of the fiber. Further cleaning is provided by picking machines which also arrange the blended fiber into parallel strands wound into large rolls (laps). Laps usually weigh from 60 to 90 pounds and are lifted (doffed) into trucks for transport to the carding operation. At carding, the fiber is further straightened, cleaned, paralleled into loose rope-like strands called card sliver, and coiled into drums. In the next operation, drawing frames tighten alignment and uniformity. Roving machines further thin the strands, twist them for strength and firmness, and wind them onto bobbins. Spinning is the final stage in yarn manufacture. The strands are drawn out still further and twisted tightly to form the yarn. The yarn is rewound onto the small bobbins.

In a vertically integrated mill, the yarn is further processed into cloth. The winding and warping operations transfer the yarn from the small spinning bobbins onto larger bobbins for use in the knitting and weaving operations. During the weaving process, crosswise (filling) threads are mixed with lengthwise (warp) threads on a loom to produce cloth. Almost one-half of the operators employed in an integrated mill are weavers.[2] The woven cloth may then be finished by dyeing, bleaching, shrinking, printing, texturing, or other special processes.[3]

Although a number of the operations described in the above are mechanical, many of the lifting, transferring, feeding, and cleaning (sweeping and janitorial) operations are manual and employ unskilled workers. Semi-skilled workers have typically tended the machines with skilled fixers holding maintenance and repair jobs. The present direction in modernization has been to automate the unskilled operations, improve machine speeds, and enhance product quality. In 1985, capital expenditures totaled almost $2 billion, up from $660 million in 1965. (Table II-1). Highlights of these modernization efforts have included automatic doffing of laps from picking to carding, chutefed carding which eliminates the picking operation, open-end spinning which bypasses roving and winding by spinning card sliver in a rotor allowing for automatic winding onto bobbins, and shuttleless weaving (air and water jet), which can produce more than double previous cloth output. By 1980, shuttleless looms accounted for 15 percent of the active looms and 30 percent of the cloth production in the industry.[4]

Table II-2 shows the impact of modernization on the textile industry. Industrial production in early 1985 was 31.2 percent higher than in 1967, despite a decrease of 25.4 percent in employment. For all manufacturing, production rose to 67.1 percent and employment rose 1.4 percent from 1967 to 1985. A productivity index has been calculated to reflect the change in production with respect to employment. A comparison of this productivity index between the textile industry and all manufacturing shows that the relative gain in productivity for textiles is higher, 75.9 versus 64.8 percent for the period 1967 to 1985. Considering that automation in textiles is in its infancy, productivity will certainly continue to improve and outpace other industries.

Future gains in productivity will likely result from the implementation of robotics and electronic process control in textile manufacturing. Computers have been miniaturized to minicomputers, microcomputers, and to microprocessors (one or two function computer chips not much larger than a penny). Use of electronic process

---

[2] Richard L. Rowan, *The Negro in the Textile Industry* (Philadelphia: Industrial Research Unit, The Wharton School, University of Pennsylvania 1970), p. 10.

[3] For a more complete description of the textile production process, see U.S. Bureau of Labor Statistics, *Technology and Manpower in the Textile Industry of the 1970's*, Bulletin No. 1578 (Washington: Government Printing Office), 1968.

[4] Unpublished data, U.S. Bureau of Labor Statistics, Division of Technological Studies, Office of Productivity and Technology.

TABLE II-1

New Plant and Equipment Expenditures
1965–1985
(in billions of dollars)

Year	All Manufacturing	Durable Goods	Textile Industry
1965	$ 23.44	$ 11.50	$ .66
1966	28.20	14.06	.82
1967	28.51	14.06	.68
1968	28.37	14.12	.53
1969	31.68	15.96	.63
1970	31.95	15.80	.56
1971	29.99	14.15	.61
1972	31.35	15.64	.73
1973	38.01	19.25	.77
1974	46.01	22.62	.84
1975	47.95	21.84	.66
1976	52.48	23.68	.81
1977	60.16	27.77	.92
1978	67.62	31.66	1.04
1979	98.68	51.07	1.50
1980	115.81	58.91	1.62
1981	126.79	61.84	1.56
1982	119.68	56.44	1.33
1983	116.20	53.08	1.55
1984	138.38	65.95	1.92
1985	153.63	75.01	1.96

Source: U.S. Department of Commerce, Bureau of Economic Analysis, *Business Statistics 1979, Supplement to the Survey of Current Business; Survey of Current Business,* (Jan. 1981, Jan. 1982, Jan. 1983, Jan. 1984, Apr. 1985). Data for 1983, 1984, and 1985 are from revised tables as explained in the Feb. 1985 issue of *Survey of Current Business.*

control by microprocessors is increasing significantly and can be found regulating and monitoring fiber lengths, filament counts, spinfinish levels, and energy usage. Design of technology has begun for use in dyehouse control and scheduling, yield and heatset control on tenter frames, and doff and jambreak detection in texturing. This means that the large firms will pioneer the applications with the small firms growing more vulnerable to competition.

LOCATION OF THE INDUSTRY

Table II-3 shows the heavy concentration of textile employment in the southeastern part of the United States. Table II-4 shows that the Southeast employed approximately 70 percent of the U.S. textile labor force in 1983. New England, once the predominant manufac-

TABLE II-2

Industrial Production and Productivity
1965–1985
(percents, 1967=100)

Year	All Manufacturing			Textiles		
	Index of Industrial Production	Employment	Productivity[1]	Index of Industrial Production	Employment	Productivity[1]
1965	89.7	92.9	96.6	92.8	96.7	96.0
1966	97.9	98.8	99.1	98.4	100.6	97.8
1967	100.0	100.0	100.0	100.0	100.0	100.0
1968	106.4	101.7	104.6	107.9	103.8	103.9
1969	111.0	103.7	107.0	112.6	104.6	107.6
1970	106.4	99.6	106.8	111.8	101.8	109.8
1971	108.2	95.8	112.9	116.5	99.7	116.9
1972	118.9	98.5	120.7	132.7	102.9	129.0
1973	129.8	103.6	125.3	142.9	105.4	135.6
1974	129.4	103.2	125.4	132.8	100.7	131.9
1975	116.3	94.2	123.5	122.3	90.6	135.0
1976	130.3	97.7	133.4	134.6	95.9	140.4
1977	138.4	101.2	136.8	134.4	95.0	141.5
1978	146.8	105.4	139.3	137.5	93.8	146.6
1979	153.6	108.3	141.8	145.0	92.7	156.4
1980	146.7	104.3	140.7	138.6	88.4	156.8
1981	150.4	103.7	145.0	135.7	86.3	157.2
1982	137.6	96.6	142.4	124.5	78.2	159.2
1983	148.2	95.1	155.8	140.8	77.7	181.2
1984	164.8	100.7	163.6	138.6	78.6	176.3
1985 (Mar.)	167.1	101.4	164.8	131.2	74.6	175.9

[1] Computed by (Index of Industrial Production/Employment) ×100.
Source: U.S. Department of Commerce, Bureau of Economic Analysis, *Business Statistics*, 1979; *Survey of Current Business*, March 1981, October 1982, December 1984, May 1985.

TABLE II-3

Textile Industry Employment by Regions
1975–1983
(in thousands)

Year	United States	Northeast	Southeast	Midwest	Southwest	West
1975	906.2	177.9	626.6	62.5	9.9	29.3
1976	961.0	183.0	668.6	67.5	10.4	31.5
1977	959.2	180.9	667.7	68.4	10.4	31.8
1978	947.8	178.8	657.3	68.1	10.3	33.3
1979	929.1	169.1	654.5	63.5	9.8	32.2
1980	895.7	159.0	631.9	65.7	9.7	29.4
1981	866.2	153.8	614.4	60.5	9.3	28.2
1982	789.4	135.2	565.6	54.1	8.3	26.2
1983	780.7	129.6	563.6	53.6	7.4	26.5

Source: U.S. Department of Labor, Bureau of Labor Statistics, *Employment, Hours and Earnings, States and Areas, 1939–82* and *Supplement to Employment, Hours and Earnings, States and Areas, 1980–83.*

turer of textiles, lost its lead by 1930 when its active spindles fell to 13.5 million compared with the 19 million for the cotton growing states (Table II-5). From Tables II-3 and II-4, it can be seen that the shift away from Northeast dominance has continued into the present, although at a much slower rate.

The shift of the textile industry from the Northeast to the Southeast has been prompted by many factors. Costs have been partic-

TABLE II-4

Textile Industry Employment by Regions
1975–1983
(percents)

Year	United States	Northeast	Southeast	Midwest	Southwest	West
1975	100.0	19.6	69.2	6.9	1.1	3.2
1976	100.0	19.0	69.6	7.0	1.1	3.3
1977	100.0	18.9	69.6	7.1	1.1	3.3
1978	100.0	18.8	69.4	7.2	1.1	3.5
1979	100.0	18.2	70.4	6.8	1.0	3.5
1980	100.0	17.8	70.5	7.3	1.1	3.3
1981	100.0	17.8	70.9	7.0	1.1	3.2
1982	100.0	17.2	71.6	6.9	1.0	3.3
1983	100.0	16.6	72.2	6.9	0.9	3.4

Source: Derived from Table II-3.

TABLE II-5

Cotton-System Spindles in Place by Region
1910–1965
(in thousands)

Year	United States	Cotton Growing States	New England	All Other States
1910	29,188	10,801	16,112	2,275
1920	35,481	15,231	18,287	1,963
1930	34,025	19,122	13,479	1,424
1940	24,750	18,136	5,884	730
1950	22,995	18,244	4,332	419
1960	19,953	18,311	1,522	120
1965	19,332	18,512	756	64

Source: U.S. Bureau of the Census, *Cotton Production and Distribution,* Bulletins
110–202.

ularly important since textile demand is "highly elastic." [5] Labor, transportation, and taxes have all been cheaper in the Southeast. The move has presented opportunities to modernize production facilities. The southern labor force has been situated in rural areas where unions have been weak. These same reasons have also contributed to the present growth of new industry in the Sunbelt.[6]

Although it will be explored further in this chapter, it should be mentioned here that the industry is highly vulnerable to foreign price competition. This vulnerability is derived in part from the regional concentration of textile production. Tables II-6, II-4, and II-3 show that within the Southeast, North Carolina, South Carolina, and Georgia employed 56.4 percent of the national textile employment and 78.0 percent of the regional total in 1983. In fact, North Carolina alone employed 28.6 percent of the national total as compared to 27.8 for the Northeast, Midwest, Southwest, and West regions combined. This concentration opens the industry to potential impact by regional economic events such as the migration of new and higher wage paying industry into the region. Higher wages for the region lead to higher wages for the textile industry which in turn lead to rising prices. This eventually leads consumers to purchase cheaper foreign products. The United States textile man-

---

[5] F. Ray Marshall, *Labor in the South* (Cambridge: Harvard University Press 1967), p. 80.

[6] For further discussion, see "Business Loves the Sunbelt (And Vice Versa)," *Fortune,* Vol. 95, No. 6 (June 1977) pp. 132–144; "The New Rich South: Frontier for Growth," *Business Week,* No. 2242 (September 2, 1972), pp. 30–37; "The Second War Between the States," *Business Week,* No. 2432 (May 17, 1976), pp. 92–114.

Employee Relations in the Textile Industry

TABLE II-6

Textile Industry Employment in North Carolina, South Carolina,
and Georgia
1975–1983

Year	United States (000s)	(%)	North Carolina (000s)	(%)	South Carolina (000s)	(%)	Georgia (000s)	(%)
1975	906.2	100.0	247.3	27.3	137.3	15.2	111.2	12.3
1976	961.0	100.0	257.0	26.7	149.5	15.6	121.1	12.6
1977	959.2	100.0	257.8	26.9	146.3	15.3	123.1	12.8
1978	947.8	100.0	255.3	26.9	143.4	15.1	123.7	13.0
1979	929.1	100.0	253.5	27.3	142.1	15.3	123.7	13.3
1980	895.7	100.0	245.8	27.4	136.9	15.3	117.6	13.1
1981	866.2	100.0	238.1	27.5	132.5	15.3	113.6	13.1
1982	789.4	100.0	223.2	28.3	117.5	14.9	102.2	12.9
1983	780.7	100.0	223.6	28.6	113.6	14.6	103.1	13.2

Source: U.S. Department of Labor, Bureau of Labor Statistics, *Employment, Hours and Earnings, States and Areas,* 1939–82 and *Supplement to Employment, Hours and Earnings, States and Areas,* 1980–83.

ufacturers will either adapt through productivity gains or fold. Both of these results are now occurring.

EMPLOYMENT OVERVIEW

Employment figures in the United States textile industry have been steadily falling as shown in Table II-3. For the period 1975 to 1983, employment fell from 906,200,000 to 780,700,000 for a decrease of 13.8 percent. The decline is more pronounced if the comparison is made between 1976 and 1983. This decline reflects the industry's efforts to find alternatives to rising labor costs. Jobs are being eliminated through automation and plant closings. An alternative, which has not been adapted by the industry, is the relocation of manufacturing facilities overseas to take advantage of cheaper labor. A final and growing alternative is corporate diversification. As the competitive nature of the textile environment changes because of higher domestic labor costs and the increasing influx of imports produced in cheaper labor markets under foreign government subsidy, textile firms are reconsidering expansions in the industry. Some companies are experimenting with diversification away from low margin textiles into other industries. Therefore, jobs that would normally be available through industry expansion, which could accommodate jobs lost to automation or modernization, are not realized.

TABLE II-7

Textile Industry Occupational Distribution
1966–1984
(percents)

Occupational Group	1966	1970	Year 1975	1979	1984
Officials and Managers	5.1	6.0	7.4	7.6	7.8
Professionals	0.9	1.2	1.5	1.6	2.3
Technicians	1.0	1.2	1.7	2.0	2.5
Sales Workers	0.8	0.9	0.9	1.2	1.1
Office and Clerical	6.4	6.8	6.9	6.8	6.9
Total White-collar	14.2	16.1	18.4	19.2	20.6
Craftsmen	14.4	13.7	14.4	14.5	15.3
Operatives	57.8	56.8	55.1	53.8	53.2
Laborers	11.5	11.2	9.8	10.2	8.7
Total Blue-collar	83.7	81.7	79.3	78.5	77.2
Service Workers	2.1	2.2	2.3	2.3	2.2

Source: Derived from *Equal Employment Opportunity Reports* 1966 No. 1; 1970 Vol. I; 1975 Vol. I; and 1979, 1984, Wharton Industrial Research Unit EEO Data Bank. (EEO data cover only those companies with 100 or more employees).

Occupational Distribution

The United States textile labor force is predominantly blue collar. Table II-7 shows that in 1984, 77.2 percent of textile employment was classified as blue-collar. Within this blue-collar classification, and consistent with the earlier discussion of technology, semi-skilled operatives dominate with 53.2 percent (1984) of total employment and 68.9 percent (1984) of the blue-collar figure.

Consistent with earlier discussion, however, Table II-7 also shows a decline in the ratio of blue-collar labor to white-collar employees. This decline is mainly the result of automation and plant closings. Automation in textiles is eliminating Operative positions at a faster rate than white-collar positions. This may also indicate that textile firms are already lean with respect to white-collar labor and potential labor savings are only available in the blue-collar workforce.

A concluding note on occupational distribution is the low Sales Workers percentage indicated in Table II-7. This small percentage (1.1 percent for 1984) is indicative of the industrial nature of textile products. The industry predominantly manufactures materials used in the production of such items as apparel, automobile tires, surgical dressings, and tennis ball covers. Large sales staffs are not required, since the number of textile product consumers is relatively small.

Race/Sex Distribution

The textile industry is employing more women and minorities than at any time in the past. As shown in Table II-8, the employment of nonwhite males has increased in major occupational categories with the most dramatic gains in the white-collar fields. The decline in the representation of nonwhite males in the Laborers and Service Workers categories may be looked upon as a positive change since, presumably, more job opportunities have been opened in the Crafts-men and Operative positions. This has allowed an upgrading of nonwhites into more highly skilled areas. Nonwhite females have paralleled this growth, although this group has also shown dramatic increases in the blue-collar occupations as well. Table II-8 also il-lustrates the exodus of white males from the industry, with a shift of white females from Crafts and Operatives positions to fill the vacancies left by white males in the Professionals and Managers categories, and ultimately, the employment of minorities in the jobs vacated by white females. As already mentioned, this compositional shift is the result of higher paying industry attracting white males away from textiles. The industry is therefore challenged to seek out and train replacements. The industry has contributed significantly to the sharp rise in real personal income in the Southeast[7] by enlisting more and more previously unemployed women and mi-norities and training them for manufacturing jobs.

Hours of Employment

Production worker average gross weekly hours for each SIC Code within the textile industry is presented in Table II-9. As these data show, average hours of employment have fallen for the industry from 41.5 in 1975 to 39.4 in 1984. This reflects a net change of −5.1 percent. This decline is shared by all subclassifications within the industry except for a small increase in SIC 229. Broad Woven Fabric Mills (223) showed the least net change at −0.1 percent and Yarn and Thread Mills (228) showed the greatest net change at −8.3 percent.

Earnings

Textile wages have always lagged behind most other industries (Table II-10). This lag is attributed to several factors. Two of these factors are described below. The first and most important factor is

---

[7] "The Second War Between the States," *Business Week*, No. 2432 (May 17, 1976), pp. 92–114.

TABLE II-8

Textile Industry Employment by Race, Sex, and Occupation
1966–1984
(percents)

	Year	Officials & Managers	Professionals	Technicians	Sales Workers	Office & Clerical	Craftsmen	Operatives	Laborers	Service Workers
White Male	1966	95.0	92.6	75.5	89.4	25.5	75.1	38.7	53.6	57.1
	1970	94.6	89.4	70.9	83.1	21.4	73.2	32.5	45.8	51.3
	1975	90.4	82.4	61.4	78.1	17.2	72.0	28.6	41.7	47.0
	1979	85.6	76.8	54.0	63.1	14.2	69.9	27.1	38.5	45.1
	1984	82.2	62.4	50.2	65.2	13.6	66.5	26.8	41.1	42.6
White Female	1966	4.4	6.7	23.0	10.0	72.2	21.5	53.3	21.6	12.0
	1970	4.1	9.2	24.8	16.1	74.0	18.8	50.3	25.3	15.3
	1975	6.2	14.4	31.3	19.9	75.4	15.6	45.7	25.3	15.9
	1979	9.0	18.4	35.3	32.5	76.1	14.2	43.6	24.5	17.1
	1984	11.3	28.9	36.1	30.9	74.7	15.8	42.2	24.5	19.7
Nonwhite Male	1966	0.4	0.6	1.3	0.4	1.2	2.1	5.2	21.2	24.3
	1970	1.2	1.0	3.3	0.6	1.9	5.1	9.0	22.4	24.9
	1975	3.1	2.5	4.4	1.0	2.8	9.1	11.8	23.9	25.4
	1979	4.6	3.4	6.2	1.9	3.1	11.9	12.9	25.1	24.6
	1984	5.2	3.4	6.6	1.6	3.3	12.7	13.1	23.1	22.3
Nonwhite Female	1966	0.1	0.1	0.2	0.2	1.1	1.3	2.8	3.6	6.6
	1970	0.1	0.4	1.0	0.2	2.7	2.9	8.2	6.5	8.5
	1975	0.3	0.7	2.9	1.0	4.6	3.3	13.9	9.1	11.7
	1979	0.8	1.4	4.5	2.5	6.6	4.0	16.4	11.9	13.2
	1984	1.4	5.3	7.1	2.3	8.4	5.0	17.9	11.3	15.4

Source: Derived from *Equal Employment Opportunity Reports* 1966 No. 1 Part II; 1970 Vol. I; 1975 Vol. I; 1979 and 1984 Wharton Industrial Research Unit EEOC Data Bank.

TABLE II-9

Production Worker Average Gross Weekly Hours, Textile Industry
1975–1984 (at December each year)

Year	SIC Codes[1]									
	22	221	222	223	224	225	226	227	228	229
1975	41.5	42.6	41.7	42.1	41.8	39.0	44.0	41.6	42.0	42.4
1980	40.8	41.6	41.1	41.5	41.1	38.7	42.6	42.3	40.8	42.9
1984	39.4	39.4	40.0	41.8	39.7	37.5	41.2	40.8	38.5	42.9

Source: U.S. Bureau of Labor Statistics, U.S. Department of Labor, *Employment &
Earnings,* (March 1983, 1984, 1985).
[1] *Note:* The Standard Industrial Classification codes are as follows: 22, Textile Mill
Products; 221, Broad Woven Fabric Mills, Cotton; 222, Broad Woven Fabric
Mills, Man-made Fiber and Silk; 223, Broad Woven Fabric Mills, Wool (in-
cluding Dyeing and Finishing); 224, Narrow Fabrics and Other Smallwares
Mills; 225, Knitting Mills; 226, Dyeing and Finishing Textiles, Except Wool
Fabrics and Knit Goods; 227, Floor Covering Mills; 228, Yarn and Thread
Mills; and 229, Miscellaneous Textile Goods.

the labor intensity of the industry. Labor costs play a more significant role in manufacturing costs in textiles than in capital intensive
industries. Increases in wages are either passed on to the customer
or absorbed as reductions to profit. Because of the import pressure
(described later in this chapter), textiles are finding it difficult to
increase sales prices to cover higher production costs. Therefore, to
ensure some measure of profitability, wages are increased very
slowly. A second factor is the predominance of unskilled and semi-
skilled labor in the industry. Most jobs are manual, repetitive, and
require no previous training.

TABLE II-10

Production Worker Hourly Earnings, Selected Industries
1975–1984
(at December each year)

SIC Code	Industry	1975	1980	1981	1982	1983	1984
22	Textiles	$3.55	$5.33	$5.72	$ 6.03	$ 6.31	$ 6.57
23	Apparel	3.27	4.81	5.05	5.26	5.46	5.65
28	Chemicals	5.61	8.08	9.52	10.34	10.89	11.37
30	Rubber/Plastics	4.51	6.89	7.48	7.89	8.18	8.40
34	Fabricated Metals	5.29	7.86	8.53	8.97	9.38	9.55
35	Machinery	5.62	8.57	9.20	9.41	9.91	10.16
36	Electrical	4.78	7.39	7.93	8.45	8.86	9.27
	Average	4.66	7.08	7.63	8.05	8.43	8.71

Source: U.S. Bureau of Labor Statistics, U.S. Department of Labor, *Employment and
Earnings* (March 1976, 1981, 1983, 1984, 1985).

TABLE II-11

*Textile Industry Production Worker Average Hourly Earnings
Selected SIC Codes
1975–1984 (as of December each year)*

Year	22	221	222	223	224	225	226	227	228	229
				SIC Codes[1]						
1975	$3.55	$3.63	$3.69	$3.67	$3.33	$3.37	$3.88	$3.65	$3.33	$3.82
1980	5.33	5.51	5.56	5.39	4.81	4.95	5.74	5.54	5.00	5.93
1981	5.72	5.93	6.04	5.87	5.29	5.27	6.17	5.87	5.37	6.30
1982	6.03	6.33	6.42	6.27	5.71	5.51	6.45	6.21	5.65	6.67
1983	6.31	6.53	6.72	6.61	5.99	5.78	6.75	6.56	5.92	7.05
1984	6.57	6.78	7.01	6.88	6.20	6.05	7.02	6.71	6.10	7.39

Source: U.S. Bureau of Labor Statistics, U.S. Department of Labor, *Employment and Earnings* (March 1976, 1981, 1983, 1984, 1985).
[1] *Note:* See Table II-9 for code specifications.

Table II-11 shows the production worker average hourly earnings for each SIC Code within the industry. As this table shows, in 1984, Knitting Mills (225) workers earned on average the least ($6.05 per hour), and Miscellaneous Textile Goods (229) workers earned on average the most ($7.39 per hour). In terms of net change over the period 1975 to 1984, average hourly earnings for Man-made Fiber and Silk Mills (222) and Miscellaneous Textile Goods (229) workers showed the greatest with increases of 90 and 93 percent, respectively, and Narrow Fabrics and Other Smallwares Mills (224) workers showed the least with an increase of 77 percent.

Turnover

Labor turnover in the textile industry is presented in Table II-12. For the period 1970 to 1981, both accessions and separations per 100 employees have fallen for net changes of −27.2 percent and −9.7 percent, respectively. The reduction in both these figures indicates a general contraction in industry employment. As the industry becomes smaller and leaner, many of the marginal employees who are subject to high turnover are separated, leaving fewer potential turnover candidates.

The general contraction is made more apparent by comparing the absolute accession and separation rates. The net effect is fewer employees. An interesting note is that the rates presented do not appear to have stabilized, indicating further declines.

TABLE II-12

Labor Turnover in the Textile Industry
1965–1981

Year	Accessions/ 100 Employees	Separations/ 100 Employees
1965	4.4	4.1
1970	4.9	5.5
1975	4.5	4.7
1980	3.7	4.1
1981	3.2	3.7

Source: U.S. Bureau of Labor Statistics, U.S. Department of Labor, *Employment and Earnings,* (March 1966, 1971, 1981, 1982). (Beginning in 1983, these data are not included in *Employment and Earnings*).

THE PROBLEM OF IMPORTS

In previous sections, the pressure of imports has been referred to as a justification for trends such as automation, diversification, slow wage increases, employment declines, and industry contraction and centralization. This import pressure is defined as the availability of cheaper textile and apparel products from foreign producers.[8] Table II-13 illustrates the increase in textile imports. Textile product imports increased 428 percent from $795 million in 1965 to $4,200 million in 1984. Cotton fabric imports increased 512 percent from $133.7 million in 1965 to $819.1 million in 1984. Current

TABLE II-13

Textile Imports
1965–1984
(in millions of dollars)

Year	Textile Yarn, Fabric, and Related Products	Cotton Fabric	Wool Fabric
1965	$ 795.2	$ 133.7	$ 105.2
1970	1,135.4	173.2	74.4
1975	1,233.5	221.4	31.6
1980	2,504.1	436.3	67.8
1984[1]	4,200.0	819.1	145.0

Source: U.S. Bureau of Census, FT135: *U.S. General Imports, Schedule A, Commodity by Country,* December 1970, 1975, 1980, and November 1984; FT125: *U.S. Imports of Merchandise for Consumption,* December 1965.
[1] Figures for 1984 include only January through November 1984.

---

[8] Since the apparel industry is the predominant user of textile products, any reduction in apparel business will certainly result in a loss of market to the textile industry.

predictions are for a 7 to 10 percent annual increase in textile and apparel imports, while domestic consumer demand will only grow at 2 to 3 percent annually. This will result in a 10 percent decline in market share for the United States textile industry.[9]

Negotiated import restrictions have been pursued by the United States government with foreign producers. The purpose of limitation agreements is not to inflate domestic prices, but to ensure that modernization plans within the industry have an opportunity to mature. One such agreement, which went into effect on January 1, 1974, was the Multifiber Arrangement (MFA). This agreement provides the basis for negotiating bilateral trade agreements. As initially drafted, the MFA required that foreign producers restrict import growth to an annualized rate of 6 percent with flexibility such that the growth rate could reach 24 percent in any given year (by borrowing quota from another year). To date, this agreement has failed to achieve its objectives. The United States government is now pushing for import quotas tied to domestic market growth with special interest groups also advocating surge limitations to prevent disruptive quota borrowing.

Recent congressional testimony by trade union leaders and corporate officials highlights the real and potential employment effects of textile imports. Sol. C. Chaikin, former President of the International Ladies' Garment Workers Union, has said that "American workers are still losing their jobs because 'textile mills and garment shops in our country are curtailing production or closing down altogether' as a result of rising imports." [10] Jack Sheinkman, Secretary-Treasurer of the Amalgamated Clothing and Textile Workers Union, testified that "100,000 textile and apparel jobs were lost in 1984, employment is down 250,000 since 1980, and 'there are almost half a million fewer textile and apparel workers today than when the Multifiber Arrangement went into effect in 1974.' " [11] These statements were made in support of bipartisan legislation that would expand the list of covered textile and apparel products and limit import growth to between 1 percent and 6 percent annually. Carlos Moore, Executive Vice President of the American Textile Manufacturers Institute, testified at the same hearings on behalf of 19 trade associations in the industry, indicating that the government's "textile import program is seriously flawed." [12]

---

[9] "More Gloom for U.S. Textiles," *Business Week,* No. 2580 (April 9, 1979), pp. 66.

[10] *AFL-CIO News,* Vol. 30, No. 29 (July 20, 1985), p. 5.

[11] *Ibid.*

[12] Bureau of National Affairs, *Daily Labor Report,* #45, (March 7, 1985), page E-5.

Roger Milliken, President of Milliken and Company, has become the principal spokesman for "Crafted With Pride Council, an industry-union coalition that is trying to win sympathy for the battered textile industry." [13] In an uncharacteristic role, Milliken and other industry leaders find themselves in agreement with the unions which are pushing for import restrictions. Milliken has been a major spokesman for fair competition but he has said that " 'Free trade' is an obsolete definition of today's world. America is sacrificing its manufacturing infrastructure on the alter of free trade, a God no other country worships." [14]

Milliken's position is further buttressed by economist, Robert Kuttner, who states:

> The reality is that nowhere are the textile and apparel markets creatures of free trade. For 20 years a complex market-sharing pact known as the Multifibers Agreement has regulated the rate of growth of textile imports to Western Europe and the U.S. . . . Despite the Multifibers Agreement, Third World production soared ... Such Asian textile exporters as Korea, Taiwan, the Philippines, Singapore, and that paragon of laissez-faire, China, not only subsidize development of their textile industries but also stringently protect their home textile markets against one another. You can't find a Korean shirt in Taiwan, or vice versa. Some free traders. [15]

According to the American Textile Manufacturers Institute (ATMI), total textile and apparel imports into the United States in 1980 amounted to 4.8 billion square yard equivalents and, in the following years, the figures were as follows: 1981—5.8 billion; 1982—5.9 billion; 1983—7.7 billion; and in 1984—10.2 billion. (Table II-14 and Figure II-2). ATMI estimates that for every one billion square yards of textile and apparel imports, 100,000 jobs are displaced in the U.S. fibers, textile, and apparel industry. The 1984 imports would be the equivalent of 1,000,000 job opportunities lost to U.S. workers.

The bill designed to limit textile imports was vetoed by President Reagan in December 1985, and the House of Representatives failed to override the veto by a 276 to 149 margin on August 6, 1986. [16]

---

[13] "Textile Imports are Swamping Even the Best Companies," *Business Week*, No. 2912 (September 16, 1985) p. 52. See also "The New Trade Strategy," *Business Week*, No. 2915 (October 7, 1985), pp. 90–96; and David L. Perlman, "Reagan Trade Plan Rejects Remedies on Job-killing Imports," *AFL-CIO News*, Vol. 30, No. 39 (September 28, 1985), pp. 1–2.

[14] Linda Williams, "Milliken and Company's Chairman Speaks Out for Textiles Manufactured in the U.S.", *The Wall Street Journal* (September 17, 1985), p. 24.

[15] Robert Kuttner, "Blind Faith in Free Trade Doesn't Pay," *Business Week*, No. 2916 (October 14, 1985), p. 22.

[16] See *Southern Textile News*, Vol. 42, No. 31 (August 11, 1986), p. 1.

TABLE II-14

U.S. Imports of Textile Manufactures
1973–1985
(millions of equivalent square yards)

Period	Cotton[1]	Man-Made Fiber[1]	Wool[2]	Total[2]
1973	1,593	3,433	99	5,125
1974	1,463	2,862	86	4,411
1975	1,281	2,470	78	3,829
1976[3]	1,924	2,954	109	4,987
1977[3]	1,639	3,195	143	4,977
1978	2,213	3,382	144	5,739
1979	1,893	2,624	122	4,639
1980	2,009	2,746	129	4,884
1981	2,574	3,067	134	5,775
1982	2,448	3,342	146	5,935
1983	2,988	4,237	184	7,409
1983*	2,988	4,531	184	7,703
1984	4,062	5,836	263	10,161
1985**	4,228	5,840	182	10,250

[1] U.S. Department of Commerce conversion factors used to convert units to square yard equivalents. [2] Wool floor covering included from 1962–1973. [3] Data Revised to conform with new 1978 textile and apparel category system. SOURCE: U.S. Department of Commerce.
* Total and man-made fiber categories include flat goods beginning 1983 and subsequent years.
** Annual rate based on first three months of 1985.

Some companies, which have not expected much import relief, have moved toward restructuring. Fieldcrest competed its acquisition of Cannon Mills in January 1986, Springs Industries has bought M. Lowenstein Corporation; West Point-Pepperell has purchased Cluett, Peabody, and Burlington Industries has negotiated a sale of its sheet and towel division to J.P. Stevens.[17] It appears that the industry is moving toward fewer but larger companies.

PRODUCT MIX

Product mix within the textile industry has shifted over time, with man-made fibers taking a leading position over cotton and wool. This is evidenced first by looking at the employment trends shown in Table II-15. Note that from 1965 to 1984, Cotton Mills (221) lost 9 percent of textile employment declining from 25 percent in 1965 to 16 percent in 1984; Wool Mills (223) lost 2 percent de-

---

[17] See *Business Week*, No. 2928 (January 13, 1986), p. 59; Scott Kilman, "Textile Companies Rapidly Stake Out Niches," *The Wall Street Journal* (February 5, 1986), p. 6, and *Textile News*, Vol. 42, No. 6 (February 10, 1986), pp. 1 and 11.

FIGURE II-2

*U.S. Imports of Textile Manufactures
(millions of equivalent square years)*

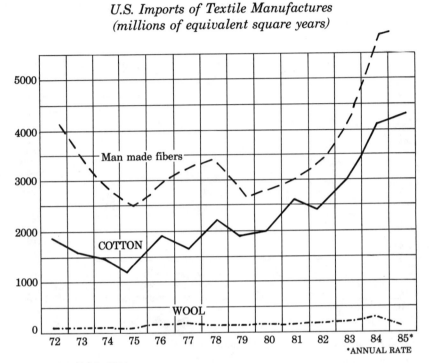

Source: See Table II-14.

clining from 5 percent in 1965 to 3 percent in 1984. These declines
are contrasted with the 2 percent gain for Man-made Fiber and Silk
Mills (222) which rose from 10 percent in 1965 to 12 percent in
1984.

TABLE II-15

*Textile Employment by Major SIC Code
1965–1984
(percents)*

	SIC Code[1]								
Year	22	221	222	223	224	225	226	227	228	229
1965	100	25	10	5	3	25	8	4	12	8
1970	100	23	10	3	3	24	9	6	14	8
1975	100	18	13	2	3	26	9	6	16	7
1980	100	17	14	2	3	26	9	6	15	8
1984	100	16	12	3	3	27	9	7	15	8

Source: Derived from U.S. Bureau of Labor Statistics, U.S. Department of Labor,
Employment and Earnings (March 1966, 1971, 1976, 1981, 1985).
[1] *Note:* See Table II-9 for code specifications.

TABLE II-16

Textile Sector Production Levels
1968–1984

Year	Fabric, Woven (gray goods)	Cotton Cloth Broadwoven	Man-made Fiber & Silk, Broadwoven	Wool & Worsted Woven Goods	Floor Covering Shipments
	millions of linear yards				millions of square yards
1968	12,709	7,476	5,204	243	601
1969	12,339	6,968	5,394	223	675
1970	11,212	6,246	5,028	179	687
1971	10,913	6,149	4,886	113	770
1972	11,048	5,616	5,567	102	943
1973	11,755	5,086	6,109	101	1,025
1974	11,054	4,714	5,923	81	939
1975	9,777	4,095	5,278	79	834
1976	10,448	4,718	6,092	97	921
1977	10,237	4,356	6,224	102	1,074
1978	10,228	4,007	6,603	117	1,162
1979	8,065	3,858	6,590	117	1,206
1980	8,420	4,456	10,744	—	1,058
1981	8,176	3,856	11,449	193	991
1982	7,118	3,794	9,760	121	886
1983	7,676	4,192	11,461	144	1,090
1984	7,154	3,978	11,875	158	1,114

Source: U.S. Department of Commerce, *Business Statistics* (1979); *Survey of Current Business* (March 1981, October 1982; January and May 1985).

Table II-16 reinforces this shift by showing that all woven goods except Man-made have experienced declines in production levels of −46.8 percent for cotton cloth, −43.8 percent for gray goods, and −35 percent for wool and worsted goods. Man-made, however, has experienced an increase in production of 128 percent from 5,204 linear yards in 1968 to 11,875 linear yards in 1984. The shift is certainly real, and reflects a trend in consumer demand from cotton and wool products to cloth produced from man-made fibers.

GOVERNMENT REGULATION

The textile industry and the government have been at odds many more times in recent years than they have been in agreement.[18] Although the two are working together to regulate and restrict

---

[18] "Textiles and Government: A Love-Hate Affair," *Textile World,* Vol. 123, No. 1 (January 1973), p. 41.

imports, the industry is opposed to its own regulation. Government regulation has arisen from directives by several agencies. The Occupational Safety and Health Administration (OSHA) has imposed noise and cotton dust standards which will cost the industry upwards of $2.7 billion to implement. The Federal Trade Commission (FTC) is regulating fabric flammability and product labeling. The Environmental Protection Agency (EPA) is monitoring effluent discharge at textile plants. The Equal Employment Opportunity Commission (EEOC) and the Civil Rights Commission (CRC) are monitoring employment practices. The National Labor Relations Board (NLRB) ensures management's compliance with union representation. And, the Security and Exchange Commission (SEC) regulates financial reporting practices.[19] The above list is by no means exhaustive, and certainly the myriad of regulations which govern the United States textile industry contribute to the industry's financial vulnerability.

SUMMARY

The United States textile industry is labor intensive with trends toward modernization and centralization under pressures of declining labor availability, rising imports, and government regulation. The textile labor force is composed mostly of unskilled and semi-skilled production workers and is shifting away from majority white male employment to include higher percentages of women and minorities. Finally, despite the centralization trend, the small firm predominates with the Southeast as its primary location.

---

[19] For further discussion see: "Can Marginal Mills Endure the Cotton Dust Standard?," *Textile World,* Vol. 128, No. 7 (July 1978), p. 23. Herbert R. Northrup, Richard L. Rowan, and Charles R. Perry, *The Impact of OSHA,* (Philadelphia: Industrial Research Unit, The Wharton School, University of Pennsylvania, 1978). "New Noise Standard Can Cost Textiles $2.7 Billion," *Textile World,* Vol. 124, No. 8 (August 1974), p. 27.

CHAPTER III

The Southern Industrial Environment

As shown in Chapter II, approximately 70 percent of the textile labor force in the United States is employed in the Southeast and, within the Southeast, 79 percent of the textile labor force is concentrated in North Carolina, South Carolina, and Georgia. This chapter examines the industrial environment in those states including regional perspectives on trends in manufacturing employment, race distribution, and cost-of-living; state perspectives on trends in race distribution; and state and county perspectives on trends in population, manufacturing employment, earnings, and new capital expenditures. Collectively, these perspectives provide a better understanding of regional industrial realignment and industrial structures in the Southeast. Regional realignment can pose a significant challenge to textile industrial relations. The textile industry will be called upon to alter its personnel policies and practices in order to compete with the new better paying and less labor intensive industries developing in the South.

THE SOUTH: A REGIONAL OVERVIEW OF MANUFACTURING EMPLOYMENT, RACE DISTRIBUTION, AND COST-OF-LIVING

Compared to other regions in the country, the South has experienced significant gains in manufacturing employment for all industries as shown in Table III-1. Indeed, in almost all industries, the Northeast and North Central regions have experienced declines in percentage of total industry for the period 1950 to 1982. The largest decline occurred in the Northeast textile industry (58 percent) and the smallest decline occurred in the North Central paper industry (13 percent). Although the West showed gains in every industry presented, these gains were not as dramatic as those that occurred in the South.

Closer examination of Table III-1 also shows that, within the South, major growth occurred in three high paying industries—

TABLE III-1

Regional Distribution of Manufacturing Employment by Selected Industries[a]

1950–1982

(Percent of Total Industry)

Industry	Northeast					North Central					South					West				
	1950	1960	1970	1977	1982	1950	1960	1970	1977	1982	1950	1960	1970	1977	1982	1950	1960	1970	1977	1982
Furniture	26	24	20	15	16	35	28	24	23	23	29	37	45	48	46	10	11	11	14	15
Stone, Clay, and Glass	34	28	28	21	23	36	35	32	26	27	21	25	28	36	34	9	12	12	17	16
Metals	37	33	29	25	26	43	39	42	44	37	13	15	19	21	24	7	13	10	10	13
Machinery	33	32	28	23	23	55	49	48	46	37	7	11	14	20	17	5	8	10	11	23
Electrical	50	41	34	27	28	42	36	33	35	25	4	12	19	24	25	4	11	14	14	22
Food	25	24	21	17	16	39	34	34	32	31	23	26	29	30	33	13	16	16	21	20
Textiles	45	32	23	20	19	4	4	3	2	3	50	63	72	76	76	1	1	2	2	2
Apparel	63	53	41	35	33	15	12	11	10	8	17	29	41	45	48	5	6	7	10	11
Paper	40	35	30	29	28	32	30	31	29	28	20	25	28	31	33	8	10	11	11	11
Chemicals	34	31	30	25	24	26	27	26	22	23	33	34	36	45	44	7	8	8	8	9
Rubber	32	35	29	26	24	49	43	42	39	34	11	12	20	23	29	8	10	9	12	13

Source: Derived from Bureau of the Census, U.S. Department of Commerce, 1950, 1960, 1970, *Census of the Population, Detailed Characteristics*, U.S.; 1977, 1982, *Census of Manufacturers*.
[a] Regional definitions by Bureau of the Census are found in Table II-4.

electrical, machinery, and rubber; and in one low paying industry—apparel. The slowest gains in percentage of total industry manufacturing employment for the South occurred in food, chemicals, and textiles. Collectively, these changes indicate that employment in the South is increasing in all industries with the fastest growth taking place in higher paying industries which have traditionally not been located in the South. In 1950, only 4 percent of the nation's electrical employment, 7 percent of the machinery employment, and 11 percent of the rubber employment were located in the South. By 1982, 25 percent of the nation's electrical employment, 16 percent of the machinery employment, and 29 percent of the rubber employment were located in the South. In addition, chemical employment grew from 33 percent in 1950 to 44 percent in 1982. Indeed, the southern industrial environment has been realigning over the past three decades, and new challenges have been presented to those who must manage the human resources function.

In addition to industrial realignment, the South is experiencing changes in its racial distribution. Table III-2 shows that less of the nation's non-white population lived in the South and West in 1980 than in 1950. In contrast, more of the non-white and less of the white population lived in the Northeast and North Central Region. For the period 1950 to 1980, the Northeast experienced a 19 percent decline in white population and a 35 percent increase in non-white population. For the same period, the South experienced a 52 percent decline in non-white population and a 15 percent increase in white population. This may be a significant factor for those in the textile industry who have depended upon the availability of a large supply of unskilled labor. Non-whites may not provide an available pool of unskilled and semi-skilled labor to the textile industry in the decades ahead.

Although there is no evidence of causal relationship between the industrial realignment and changes in race distribution, mere coincidence seems a weak explanation for the significant changes in the same direction for both. It appears that the white population is relocating in response to higher paying, higher technology industries and, partially as a result of this shift, opportunities for non-whites have opened in the food, textile, and apparel industries. This shift is demonstrated in Table II-8 where non-white males and females are shown employed in increasing numbers in white-collar, Craftsmen, and Operative positions in the textile industry.

Since earnings, new capital expenditures, and population will be examined on a state and county level, the final regional characteristic to be examined will be cost-of-living using the Consumer Price

TABLE III-2

White and Non-White Population Percent Distribution by Region [a]

1950–1980

	1950		1960		1970		1980	
	Percent White	Percent Non-White	Percent White	Percent Non-White	Percent White	Percent Non-White	Percent White	Percent Non-White
United States	100.0	100.0	100.0	100.0	100.0	100.0	100.0	100.0
Northeast	27.7	13.2	26.1	15.4	24.9	18.5	22.5	17.8
North Central	31.2	14.8	30.2	17.7	29.0	19.4	27.7	17.5
South	27.3	65.7	27.4	56.1	28.4	49.0	31.3	43.0
West	13.8	6.3	16.3	10.8	17.7	13.1	18.5	21.7

Source: Derived from Bureau of the Census, U.S. Dept. of Commerce, *1980 Census of Population and Housing—U.S. Summary; 1970 Census of Population—Detailed Characteristics; 1960 Census of Population—Negro Population, by County; 1950 Census of Population Characteristics.*

[a] Region definitions by Bureau of Census found in Table I-4.

TABLE III-3

U.S. Annual Average Consumer Price Index
1967–1982
(1967=100.0)

Year	CPI-U[a]	CPI-W[b]
1967	100.0	100.0
1975	—	161.2
1977	—	181.5
1978	195.4	195.3
1979	217.4	217.7
1980	246.8	247.0
1981	272.4	272.3
1982	289.1	288.6

Source: Bureau of Labor Statistics, U.S. Dept. of Labor, *Consumer Price Index*, Dec. 1967, Dec. 1975, Dec. 1977, April 1979, Jan. 1981, Jan. 1982, Jan. 1983.
[a] All urban consumers
[b] All urban wage earners and clerical workers.

TABLE III-4

Regional Annual Average Consumer Price Index[a]
1977–1982
(1977=100.0)

	CPI-U			
Year	Northeast	North Central	South	West
1977	100.0	100.0	100.0	100.0
1978	104.3	105.3	105.4	105.1
1979	114.7	118.2	117.4	117.3
1980	129.4	134.0	132.9	134.6
1981	143.3	146.6	147.2	148.5
1982	150.8	157.0	156.6	157.5
	CPI-W			
1977	100.0	100.0	100.0	100.0
1978	104.2	105.4	105.3	105.1
1979	114.8	118.4	117.4	117.6
1980	129.4	134.2	133.0	135.0
1981	143.1	146.8	147.4	149.0
1982	150.3	156.8	156.6	157.9

Source: Bureau of Labor Statistics, U.S. Dept. of Labor, *Consumer Price Index*, Dec. 1977, April 1979, Jan. 1980, Jan. 1981, Jan. 1982, Jan. 1983.
[a] Region definitions by Bureau of the Census found in Table I-4.

Index (CPI) as a comparative measure. Tables III-3 and III-4 present the CPI-U (all urban consumers) and CPI-W (all urban wage earners and clerical workers) for the United States and its regions, respectively. (Table III-3 uses 1967 = 100 and Table III-4 uses 1977 = 100). It should be noted that periodic changes in the method of calculation make some of the figures strictly incomparable; however, trends are consistent. As Table III-4 shows, the Northeast shows the slowest rise in the CPI while the North Central, South, and West regions have similar respective growth figures. The growth in cost-of-living for the South and West parallels the realignment to high technology, high paying industries. The slower growth in cost-of-living for the Northeast parallels the decrease in higher paying manufacturing employment for this region. The high growth in cost-of-living for the North Central region, however, does not parallel the decline in higher paying industry. This may be explained by noting in Table III-1, that, although the North Central region is losing its share of high technology, high paying industry, as of 1982 it still represented over 35 percent of the nation's machinery and metals employment, as well as large concentrations of rubber and electrical employment.

In addition to the Consumer Price Index discussed earlier, one source reports increases in real personal income at 114 percent and 106 percent for the Southeast and Southwest respectively, but only 65 percent and 66 percent for the Great Lakes and New England areas over the period 1960 to 1975.[1] This further reinforces the theory of an early southern industrial realignment.

In conclusion, the South is experiencing significant growth in high technology and high wage paying industries. Evidence supporting this statement is available from an examination of changes in manufacturing employment distribution, race distribution, and cost-of-living. The next sections will examine each of three states—North Carolina, South Carolina, and Georgia—and several selected counties in these states, for further evidence of the realignments challenging the textile industry to change its structure and its management of human resources in order to compete.

THE NORTH CAROLINA TEXTILE ENVIRONMENT

The general population for North Carolina has grown at over 11 percent per decade since 1950, with its largest growth of 15.6 percent occurring between 1970 and 1980 (Table III-5). Indeed, all of the

---

[1] "The Second War Between the States", *Business Week*, No. 2432 (May 17, 1976), pp. 92–114.

TABLE III-5

North Carolina
General Population, State and Selected Counties
1950–1980

	1950	Percent Change 1950–60	1960	Percent Change 1960–70	1970	Percent Change 1970–80	1980
State	4,061,929	12.2	4,556,155	11.5	5,082,059	15.6	5,874,429
Alamance	71,220	20.3	85,674	12.5	96,362	2.9	99,136
Cabarrus	63,783	6.8	68,137	9.5	74,629	15.1	85,895
Catawba	61,794	18.4	73,191	24.2	90,873	15.8	105,208
Cleveland	64,357	2.6	66,048	9.9	72,556	15.0	83,435
Gaston	110,836	14.7	127,074	16.8	148,415	9.5	162,568
Guilford	191,057	29.0	246,520	17.1	288,590	9.9	317,154
Johnston	65,906	-4.5	62,936	-1.9	61,737	14.4	70,599
Pitt	63,789	9.6	69,942	5.7	73,900	13.2	83,651
Randolph	50,804	21.0	61,497	24.2	76,358	20.3	91,861
Rockingham	64,816	7.4	69,629	4.0	72,402	15.2	83,426
Rutherford	46,356	-2.7	45,091	5.0	47,337	13.6	53,787
Stanly	37,130	10.1	40,873	4.8	42,822	13.3	48,517

Source: Bureau of the Census, U.S. Dept. of Commerce, 1980 *Census of Population and Housing—North Carolina;* 1950, 1960, 1970, *Census of Population, Number of Inhabitants, U.S. Summary.*

TABLE III-6

North Carolina
Manufacturing Employment for State and Selected Industries
1972–1982

	1972	1974	1976	1978	1980	1982	Percent Change 1972–82
State	756,800	789,600	756,300	807,200	820,000	781,300	3
Furniture	71,500	74,400	73,700	82,200	81,500	79,100	11
Stone, Clay, and Glass	15,400	17,400	16,100	18,300	18,200	16,000	4
Metals	19,100	22,900	21,900	25,400	26,000	24,800	30
Machinery	29,700	37,000	35,700	39,600	49,500	50,300	70
Electrical	42,400	47,300	40,000	48,300	55,300	53,200	25
Food	38,700	39,700	41,200	42,200	44,000	42,800	11
Textiles	282,900	278,300	257,000	255,300	245,800	222,700	−21
Apparel	83,800	82,900	83,100	90,000	88,000	85,600	2
Paper	19,800	21,000	20,300	21,400	21,300	21,700	10
Chemicals	31,100	37,900	36,400	37,300	39,400	37,500	21
Rubber	17,200	21,200	21,000	25,500	27,100	26,000	51

Source: U.S. Bureau of Labor Statistics, U.S. Dept. of Labor, *Employment and Earnings, States and Areas,* 1939–1982.

twelve counties selected for study which have a significant textile industry presence experienced growth between 1970 and 1980, with Alamance County showing the smallest growth at 2.9 percent and Randolph County showing the largest at over 20 percent. National population grew at 11.5 percent for 1970 to 1980, and North Carolina and nine of the twelve counties shown grew at a faster rate.[2]

With respect to manufacturing employment over a more recent period, 1972 to 1982, North Carolina experienced growth of 3 percent with some industries growing faster than others (Table III-6). Machinery led the way with an increase of 70 percent followed by rubber and metals at 51 percent and 30 percent, respectively. The only industry experiencing a decline in manufacturing employment was textiles with a loss of 21 percent. In spite of this loss, however, textiles remained the single leading manufacturing industry for the state with 28.5 percent of the total in 1982 (Table III-7). The other two leading employers for the state are apparel and furniture at 10.9 percent and 10.1 percent, respectively. Although North Carolina is still dominated by labor intensive industries, heavy invest-

---

[2] Derived from Bureau of the Census, U.S. Department of Commerce, *1980 Census of Population and Housing—U.S. Summary.*

TABLE III-7

North Carolina
Selected Industry Percents for Total Manufacturing Employment
1972–1982

Industry	1972	1974	1976	1978	1980	1982	Percent Change 1972–1982
Furniture	9.4	9.4	9.7	10.2	9.9	10.1	7
Stone, Clay, and Glass	2.0	2.2	2.1	2.3	2.2	2.0	0
Metals	2.5	2.9	2.9	3.1	3.2	3.2	28
Machinery	3.9	4.7	4.7	4.6	6.0	6.4	64
Electrical	5.6	6.0	5.3	6.0	6.7	6.8	21
Food	5.1	5.0	5.5	5.3	5.4	5.5	8
Textiles	37.4	35.2	34.0	31.5	30.0	28.5	−24
Apparel	11.1	10.5	11.0	11.2	10.7	10.9	−2
Paper	2.6	2.7	2.7	2.6	2.6	2.8	8
Chemicals	4.1	4.8	4.8	4.6	4.8	4.8	17
Rubber	2.3	2.7	2.8	3.1	3.3	3.3	43

Source: Derived from Table III-6.

ments in new technology have been made in recent decades. This growth in technology is supported by the large increase in new capital expenditures for the state from $314.4 million in 1963 to $2,588.6 million in 1982 (Table III-8). Although Table III-8 shows decreases in new capital expenditures for some counties over time, this has usually followed periods of significant increases.

These figures, coupled with the production worker hourly earnings for selected industries found in Table III-9, show that the industrial realignment in the South is reflected in changes occurring within North Carolina. Table III-9 shows that the high technology industries experiencing the most growth in employment are also the higher paying industries. Indeed, in 1982, apparel paid the lowest average hourly wage for production workers at $4.66 followed by furniture, textiles, and food. Paper, with the highest rate of $9.66 per hour was followed by chemicals, rubber, machinery, and metals, all paying over $7.00 per hour. These differentials are, of course, consistent with the significance that wages play in the manufacturing costs of labor intensive industries versus high technology industries. The impetus behind the migration of textile employees to newly established high technology and higher wage paying industries, and the subsequent challenge to textile management to fill these vacancies, arises in large measure from these differentials.

With respect to race distribution in North Carolina, Table III-10 shows that in 1950 whites represented 73.4 percent of the state's

TABLE III-8

North Carolina

New Capital Expenditures by State and Selected Counties

(in millions)

	1963	1967	Percent Change 1963-72	1972	Percent Change 1967-72	1977	Percent Change 1972-77	1982	Percent Change 1977-82
State	$ 314.4	$ 664.6	111.4	$ 989.3	48.9	$ 1345.3	36.0	$ 2588.6	92.4
Alamance	5.4	16.1	198.1	32.9	104.3	19.6	-40.4	50.8	159.2
Cabarrus	12.0	13.4	11.7	13.8	3.0	16.9	22.5	82.8	390.0
Catawba	8.0	19.4	142.5	38.7	99.5	32.1	-17.1	50.1	56.1
Cleveland	14.1	10.6	-24.8	41.0	286.8	38.3	-6.6	74.4	94.2
Gaston	19.1	42.9	124.6	50.2	17.0	45.3	-9.8	81.1	79.0
Guilford	18.1	41.9	131.5	54.9	31.0	65.2	18.8	131.6	101.8
Johnston	1.0	5.8	480.0	4.0	-31.0	6.0	50.0	25.7	328.3
Pitt	2.2	4.1	86.4	3.5	-14.6	11.1	217.1	24.4	119.8
Randolph	6.3	15.0	138.1	20.0	33.3	29.6	48.0	39.8	34.4
Rockingham	10.1	14.2	40.6	22.9	61.3	115.4	403.9	51.0	-55.8
Rutherford	5.8	6.1	5.2	7.2	18.0	16.6	130.6	20.0	20.5
Stanly	21.9	13.4	-38.8	8.3	-38.1	11.7	41.0	36.5	212.0

Source: Bureau of the Census, U.S. Dept. of Commerce. *Census of Manufactures*, 1963, 1967, 1972, 1982.

TABLE III-9

North Carolina
Average Hourly Earnings for Production Workers by
State and Selected Industries
1972–1982

	1972	1974	1976	1978	1980	1982	Percent Change 1972–1982
State Average	$ 2.77	$ 3.28	$ 3.79	$ 4.47	$ 5.37	$ 6.35	129
Furniture	2.74	3.18	3.57	4.16	4.89	5.63	105
Stone, Clay, and Glass	3.07	3.63	4.23	4.98	5.98	7.08	131
Metals	3.18	3.76	4.34	5.13	6.35	7.27	128
Machinery	3.26	3.59	4.27	5.01	5.99	7.55	132
Electrical	2.99	3.50	4.12	4.91	6.30	7.68	157
Food	2.60	3.10	3.63	4.17	5.26	5.91	127
Textiles	2.62	3.09	3.57	4.21	4.95	5.68	117
Apparel	2.16	2.58	2.94	3.44	4.10	4.66	116
Paper	3.78	4.40	5.29	6.48	7.91	9.66	156
Chemicals	3.48	4.08	4.85	5.58	6.74	8.22	136
Rubber	3.10	3.60	4.20	5.14	6.06	7.76	150

Source: U.S. Bureau of Labor Statistics, U.S. Dept. of Labor, *Employment and Earnings, States and Areas,* 1939–1982.

population versus 75.8 percent in 1980. Although this increase was larger than that experienced for the South as a region, it does not appear to be a significant change. Indeed, at first glance, Table III-10 appears to contradict the earlier discussion on the national race distribution realignment; this is not the case. Table III-10 indicates only that the in-state distribution of non-whites has not changed significantly.

NORTH CAROLINA COUNTY PROFILES

With the characteristics of North Carolina as a state in the background, Tables III-11 through III-22, as well as earlier Tables III-5, III-6, III-8 and III-9, provide population, manufacturing employment and payroll, and new capital expenditures data for each of twelve counties within the state where the textile industry is a major source of employment. A brief examination of these data for each county follows. It should be borne in mind that the counties selected for study are those where the textile industry has been concentrated over a long period of time.

TABLE III-10

White and Non-White Population Distribution
North Carolina, South Carolina, Georgia, and South[a]
1950–1980
(in percents[b])

	1950		1960		1970		1980	
	White	Non-White	White	Non-White	White	Non-White	White	Non-White
South	78.0	22.0	79.1	20.9	80.4	19.6	78.2	21.8
North Carolina	73.4	26.6	74.6	25.4	76.9	23.1	75.8	24.2
South Carolina	61.1	38.9	65.1	34.9	69.4	30.6	68.8	31.2
Georgia	69.1	30.9	71.4	28.6	74.0	26.0	72.3	27.7

Source: Derived from Bureau of the Census, U.S. Dept. of Commerce, *1980 Census of Population and Housing—U.S. Summary*; *1970 Census of Population—Detailed Characteristics*; *1960 Census of Population—Negro Population, by County*; *1950 Census of Population—Population Characteristics*.

[a] South as defined by Bureau of Census (See Table I-4).
[b] White and Non-White percents for each state and region total to 100.0 percent for each year.

TABLE III-11

Alamance County, North Carolina
Manufacturing Employment and Payroll by Selected Industry
1965–1980

	Employment[a]				Payroll[b]			
	1965	1970	1975	1980	1965	1970	1975	1980
County	21,548	26,220	20,621	22,716	22,168	36,865	38,812	66,642
Furniture	613	670	583	603	638	860	1229	1912
Stone, Clay, & Glass	e	—	105	166	e	—	224	414
Metals	—	—	20–99[c]	76[d]	—	—	e	191[d]
Machinery	314	147	279	632	362	251	669	1902
Electrical	e	e	2500–4999	1000–2499	e	e	e	e
Food	412	375	215	265	410	407	438	668
Textiles	15,364	19,080	14,988	15,613	14,030	23,542	24,557	40,192
Apparel	379	350	188	558	280	341	194	1080
Paper	239	262	257	416	192	294	475	1458
Chemicals	—	—	—	—	—	—	—	—
Rubber	—	—	—	233	—	—	—	770

Source: Bureau of the Census, U.S. Dept. of Commerce, *County Business Patterns*, 1980, 1975, 1970, 1965.
[a] Number of employees for week including March 12.
[b] First quarter only in $ thousands.
[c] SIC 33 only.
[d] SIC 34 only.
[e] Withheld to avoid disclosing information for individual companies.

Alamance County (Labor area: Burlington, North Carolina)

Although Alamance County experienced population growth exceeding state levels for the period 1950 to 1970, its growth fell to a 2.9 percent increase for the period 1970 to 1980 (Table III-5). This slow growth coincides with a 40.4 percent decrease in new capital expenditures for the period 1972 to 1977 following periods of very large increases (Table (III-8).

Table III-11 shows that Alamance is still dominated by labor intensive industries, and the recent appearance of high technology, high paying industry has only been minimal. Between 1965 and 1980 the machinery and paper industries experienced employment growth, and companies in the rubber and electrical industries entered the county. As of 1980, textile, apparel, and furniture still represented 74 percent of the manufacturing employment and 65 percent of the manufacturing payroll in the county. Burlington Industries is a leading employer in the area.

TABLE III-12

Cabarrus County, North Carolina
Manufacturing Employment and Payroll by Selected Industry
1965–1980

	Employment[a]				Payroll[b]			
	1965	1970	1975	1980	1965	1970	1975	1980
County	22,531	28,944	20,436	23,287	22,143	32,042	30,044	52,436
Furniture	—	—	—	—	—	—	—	—
Stone, Clay, & Glass	—	—	—	—	—	—	—	—
Metals	—	—	100–249[c]	288[d]	—	—	e	1002[d]
Machinery	—	—	51	79	—	—	91	229
Electrical	—	—	—	—	—	—	—	—
Food	829	744	271	303	660	857	491	947
Textiles	20,931 e	26,895 e	18,727	20,551	20,859 e	29,632 e	26,974	44,977
Apparel			515	731			483	1169 e
Paper	—	—	—	20–99	—	—	—	
Chemicals	—	—	113	128	—	—	287	495
Rubber	—	—	—	—	—	—	—	—

Source: Bureau of the Census, U.S. Dept. of Commerce. *County Business Patterns*, 1965, 1970, 1975, 1980.
[a] Number of employees for week including March 12.
[b] First quarter only in $ thousands.
[c] SIC 33 only.
[d] SIC 34 only.
[e] Withheld to avoid disclosing information for individual companies.

Cabarrus County (Labor area: Kannapolis-Concord-Salisbury, North Carolina)

Cabarrus is a county dominated by the textile industry, which in 1980 represented 88 percent of the manufacturing employment and 86 percent of the manufacturing payroll in the county (Table III-12). Although Cabarrus has experienced only a minimal influx of industry, new industry has appeared quite recently, accounting for the increase in population at 15.1 percent for the period 1970 to 1980, the increase in new capital expenditures for the period 1972 to 1982, and the increase in manufacturing employment for the period 1975 to 1980 (Tables III-5, III-8, and III-12). Cabarrus has yet to experience any major industrial realignment. Cannon Mills, recently acquired by Fieldcrest, remains the dominant employer in the area.

Catawba County (Labor area: Hickory-Newton, North Carolina)

Table III-13 shows that Catawba, a county located in western North Carolina, is relatively diverse with respect to industrial employment. Furniture leads manufacturing employment and payroll

TABLE III-13

Catawba County, North Carolina
Manufacturing Employment and Payroll by Selected Industry
1965-1980

	Employment[a]				Payroll[b]			
	1965	1970	1975	1980	1965	1970	1975	1980
County	24,198	32,291	28,571	36,924	23,051	40,906	47,916	97,721
Furniture	9141	11,796	10,457	15,384	9251	15,963	17,224	40,110
Stone, Clay								
& Glass	245	259	270	483	242	389	463	1458
Metals	187[d]	840[d]	429[d]	528[d]	179[d]	1143[d]	953[d]	1763[d]
Machinery	204	194	266	380	239	296	588	1144
Electrical	[e]	[e]	1000–2499	1000–2499	[e]	[e]	[e]	[e]
Food	387	523	359	488	423	775	834	1444
Textiles	9225	11,842	9173	9683	7793	13,131	13,090	22,920
Apparel	1798	1526	1722	2312	1354	1407	1999	4379
Paper	692	779	899	1461	699	1111	1749	4051
Chemicals	—	105	58	—	—	151	135	—
Rubber	—	1054	1155	1427	—	1097	2098	3947

Source: Bureau of the Census, U.S. Dept. of Commerce. *County Business Patterns,* 1965, 1970,
    1975, 1980.
[a] Number of employees for week including March 12.
[b] First quarter only in $ thousands.
[c] SIC 33 only.
[d] SIC 34 only.
[e] Withheld to avoid disclosing information for individual companies.

with 42 percent and 41 percent shares, respectively. The second
leading employer is textiles. Catawba and Johnston are the only
two counties studied where the textile industry is not the leading
employer.

Catawba has experienced consistent growth in general population
(Table III-5) and manufacturing employment (Table III-13). New
capital expenditures for the period 1972 to 1977 declined 17.1 percent but rose again between 1977 and 1982 by 56.1 percent. Most
of the industries shown in Table III-13 were established prior to
1965 with the exception of chemicals and rubber. Both of these were
established in 1970, but chemicals disappeared by 1980.

*Cleveland County (Labor area: Shelby-Kings Mountain, North
Carolina)*

Cleveland County has experienced growth in its general population at rates just under those of the state for the period 1960 to
1980 (Table III-5). For the period 1950 to 1960, population growth
for the county was only 2.6 percent which is the slowest growth

TABLE III-14

Cleveland County, North Carolina
Manufacturing Employment and Payroll by Selected Industry
1965–1980

	Employment[a]				Payroll[b]			
	1965	1970	1975	1980	1965	1970	1975	1980
County	12,398	14,607	13,370	15,060	12,649	20,264	23,929	45,040
Furniture	e	243	100–249	100–249	e	276	e	e
Stone, Clay, & Glass	1374	e	1000–2499	1000–2499	1459	e	e	e
Metals	—	—	20–99[d]	20–99[d]	—	—	e	e
Machinery	—	—	106	122	—	—	169	349
Electrical	—	—	100–249	250–499	—	—		
Food	570	623	762	407	543	802	1522	927
Textiles	7760	8304	7185	8174	7846	10,500	12,667	21,827
Apparel	940	1004	411	564	768	1338	499	1172
Paper	e	167	100–249	20–99	e	267	e	e
Chemicals	e	e	2500–4999	1000–2499	e	e	e	e
Rubber	—	—	—	131	—	—	—	319

Source: Bureau of the Census, U.S. Dept. of Commerce. *County Business Patterns*, 1965, 1970, 1975, 1980.
[a] Number of employees for week including March 12.
[b] First quarter only in $ thousands.
[c] SIC 33 only.
[d] SIC 34 only.
[e] Withheld to avoid disclosing information for individual companies.

experienced by any county in any decade presented between 1950 and 1980 (with the exception of Johnston's decrease for 1950 to 1970 and Rutherford's decrease for 1950 to 1960).

Paralleling the more recent growth in general population, manufacturing employment has grown 21.5 percent over the period 1965 to 1980 (Table III-14). This growth in manufacturing employment is the result of recent diversification. In 1965, only seven of the eleven manufacturing industries presented in Table III-14 were established. By 1980, the remaining four had appeared. The four new industries were all high technology, high paying industries. As a result of this diversification, textile dominance fell from 63 percent of manufacturing employment and 62 percent of manufacturing payroll in 1965 to 54 percent and 48 percent respectively in 1980. This diversification is further evidenced by noting that for three of the four years presented in Table III-8, Cleveland County ranked consistently in the top third of the counties presented for new capital expenditures.

TABLE III-15

Gaston County, North Carolina
Manufacturing Employment and Payroll by Selected Industry
1965–1980

	Employment[a]				Payroll[b]			
	1965	1970	1975	1980	1965	1970	1975	1980
County	32,538	39,159	100–299	42,302	32,659	51,044	58,497	115,858
Furniture	—	—	—	20–99	—	—	—	e
Stone, Clay, &Glass	108	121	437	529	108	179	943	1706
Metals	166[d]	379[d]	557	1329	208[d]	666[d]	1294	3743
Machinery	2801	3725	3888	5609	3177	5717	9204 e	18,211 e
Electrical	—	—	100–249	250–499	—	—		
Food	511	604	392	468	565	919	633	1426
Textiles	24,923	28,720	22,413	24,735	23,941	34,903	34,085	62,011
Apparel	1198	1516	705	1714	810	1517	994	3214
Paper	e	e	100–249	100–249	e	e	e	e
Chemicals	413	416	880	1093	680	841	2181	4408
Rubber	e	510	314	482	e	861	639	1381

Source: Bureau of the Census, U.S. Dept. of Commerce. *County Business Patterns*, 1965, 1970, 1975, 1980.
[a] Number of employees for week including March 12.
[b] First quarter only in $ thousands.
[c] SIC 33 only.
[d] SIC 34 only.
[e] Withheld to avoid disclosing information for individual companies.

Gaston County (Labor area: Charlotte-Gastonia, North Carolina)

In 1965, Gaston County was dominated by the textile industry which accounted for 77 percent of the manufacturing employment and 73 percent of the manufacturing payroll (Table III-15). By 1980, however, the small industries of 1965 had experienced major growth and textiles only accounted for 58 percent of the manufacturing employment and 54 percent of the manufacturing payroll. The industries showing significant growth over the 1965 to 1980 period were metals, machinery, and chemicals. Again, these are high technology and high wage paying industries. Gaston's industrial realignment is a harbinger of events to come in those counties which have experienced only recent establishment of new industry.

Guilford County (Labor area: Greensboro-Winston-Salem-High Point, North Carolina)

Like Gaston County, Guilford County has experienced consistent growth in general population (Table III-5), and comparatively high levels of capital expenditures (Table III-8). In contrast, however,

TABLE III-16

Guilford County, North Carolina
Manufacturing Employment and Payroll by Selected Industry
1965–1980

	Employment[a]				Payroll[b]			
	1965	1970	1975	1980	1965	1970	1975	1980
County	48,799	58,410	51,376	57,628	52,356	90,011	110,764	203,895
Furniture	8085	8703	8208	9199	8548	12,013	13,588	23,438
Stone, Clay & Glass	973	1228	989	839	1251	2099	2249	2949
Metals	2426	2816[d]	3333	2876[d]	2829	4471[d]	7492	9365[d]
Machinery	1237	2507	2451	3366	1674	4458	6472	12,375
Electrical	[e]	2204	2045	1243	[e]	4834	5495	4196
Food	3012	2492	1946	2383	3222	3613	3853	7736
Textiles	15,767	16,536	12,789	11,004	14,586	20,852	21,557	32,271
Apparel	4153	4361	1917	2325	3112	4620	2664	4700
Paper	1276	1304	1186	1579	1515	2036	2351	4657
Chemicals	1398	1715	2026	2206	2044	3297	5722	9472
Rubber	817	778	1034	1640	706	1002	1776	4265

Source: Bureau of the Census, U.S. Dept. of Commerce. *County Business Patterns,* 1965, 1970, 1975, 1980.
[a] Number of employees for week including March 12.
[b] First quarter only in $ thousands.
[c] SIC 33 only.
[d] SIC 34 only.
[e] Withheld to avoid disclosing information for individual companies.

Guilford County has been diversified much longer and more evenly than Gaston County. In 1965, the three leading industries—textiles, furniture, and apparel—accounted for only 57 percent of the county's manufacturing employment and 50 percent of its manufacturing payroll. By 1980, this representation had fallen to 39 percent and 30 percent, respectively. Indeed, in 1980, seven of the eleven industries shown in Table III-16 employed over 2,000 employees each, and all but stone, clay, and glass employed over 1,000.

In addition to industrial diversity, Guilford County stands unique among the North Carolina counties presented because of its 30 percent decline in textile employment over the period 1965 to 1980. Nine of the eleven remaining counties showed increases over this period, with two showing small declines. Guilford County's textile management has certainly been challenged to maintain a stable labor base in an apparently competitive labor market.

Johnston County (Labor area: Smithfield, North Carolina)

As mentioned earlier, Johnston County is only one of the two counties selected where textiles was not the leading employer in

TABLE III-17

Johnston County, North Carolina
Manufacturing Employment and Payroll by Selected Industry
1965–1980

	Employment[a]				Payroll[b]			
	1965	1970	1975	1980	1965	1970	1975	1980
County	3265	5255	6154	9224	2652	5817	8983	22,652
Furniture	e	e	100–249	100–249	e	e	e	e
Stone, Clay, & Glass	—	e	100–249	—	—	e	e	—
Metals	—	—	—	100–249	—	—	—	e
Machinery	—	—	—	97	—	—	—	208
Electrical	e	1749	2031	4121	e	2120	3229	10,960
Food	285	309	285	360	275	399	523	869
Textiles	563	758	1332	1516	535	1037	1802	3955
Apparel	976	1764	1413	998	599	1622	1876	1866
Paper	—	—	—	—	—	—	—	e
Chemicals	—	—	—	500–999	—	—	—	e
Rubber	—	—	—	20–99	—	—	—	e

Source: Bureau of the Census, U.S. Dept. of Commerce. *County Business Patterns,* 1965, 1970, 1975, 1980.
[a] Number of employees for week including March 12.
[b] First quarter only in $ thousands.
[c] SIC 33 only.
[d] SIC 34 only.
[e] Withheld to avoid disclosing information for individual companies.

1980. Table III-17 shows that in 1980 the electrical industry was the leading employer, representing 45 percent of the manufacturing employment and 48 percent of the manufacturing payroll. Other industries which have only recently located in Johnston County have not had a significant impact on the labor market and have been accompanied by low new capital expenditures (Table III-8). Indeed, Johnston County has shared the bottom with Pitt County in terms of new capital expenditures for the four individual years reported.

Johnston County's slow growth has been further aggravated by decreases in general population for the periods 1950 to 1960 and 1960 to 1970 (Table III-5). In spite of its 14.4 percent increase in general population for the period 1970 to 1980, it appears unlikely that Johnston County will experience any significant economic changes in the next few years.

Pitt County (Labor area: Greenville, North Carolina)

It is deceiving to note that Pitt County, located in the eastern North Carolina tobacco country, has experienced consistent in-

Employee Relations in the Textile Industry

TABLE III-18

Pitt County, North Carolina
Manufacturing Employment and Payroll by Selected Industry
1965–1980

	Employment[a]				Payroll[b]			
	1965	1970	1975	1980	1965	1970	1975	1980
County	2373	4497	5781	6945	2273	5401	10,277	21,794
Furniture	—	—	—	—	—	—	—	—
Stone, Clay, & Glass	—	—	—	62	—	—	—	135
Metals	—	—	—	—	—	—	—	—
Machinery	—	180	482	720	—	285	1032	1834
Electrical	e	e	250–499	500–999	e	e	e	e
Food	270	323	636	197	231	396	1320	488
Textiles	e	e	1213	1000–2499	e	e	1969	e
Apparel	e	1419	1196	693	e	1103	1381	1567
Paper	—	—	—	500–999	—	—	e	e
Chemicals	—	—	500–999	1000–2499	—	—	—	—
Rubber	—	—	—	—	—	—	—	—

Source: Bureau of the Census, U.S. Dept. of Commerce. *County Business Patterns,* 1965, 1970, 1975, 1980.
[a] Number of employees for week including March 12.
[b] First quarter only in $ thousands.
[c] SIC 33 only.
[d] SIC 34 only.
[e] Withheld to avoid disclosing information for individual companies.

creases in general population (Table III-5) and manufacturing employment (Table III-18) and a 120 percent rise in new capital expenditures for the period 1972 to 1982 (Table III-9), since in 1980 manufacturing employment totalled only 6,945 for the whole county. Small absolute changes over a small base have appeared as significant relative net changes. As Table III-18 shows, Pitt County has a small manufacturing base led by textiles and followed by chemicals. Like Johnston County, Pitt has significant room for economic expansion.

Randolph County (Labor area: Greensboro-Winston-Salem-High Point-Ashboro, North Carolina)

Randolph County is another North Carolina county which demonstrates the industrial realignment occurring in the South and in the state. Randolph County has experienced consistent growth in general population (Table III-5) significantly exceeding state growth levels, consistent growth in new capital expenditures (Table III-9) generally exceeding state growth levels, and a 50.0 percent increase in manufacturing employment for the period 1965 to 1980. Fur-

TABLE III-19

Randolph County, North Carolina
Manufacturing Employment and Payroll by Selected Industry
1965–1980

	Employment[a]				Payroll[b]			
	1965	1970	1975	1980	1965	1970	1975	1980
County	14,059	18,273	17,073	21,097	13,228	23,537	31,615	52,865
Furniture	1412	2058	2396	4318	1200	2428	4326	9895
Stone, Clay, & Glass	—	—	—	91	—	—	—	265
Metals	—	161[d]	224[d]	398[d]	—	319[d]	610[d]	1277[d]
Machinery	—	—	60	133	—	—	132	499
Electrical	923	e	1000–2499	1000–2499	1164	e	e	e
Food	271	400	647	702	286	548	1081	1771
Textiles	8800	10,889	8310	8957	8527	14,129	15,519	21,393
Apparel	906	1422	1365	1678	581	1399	2026	3115
Paper	e	e	100–249	250–499	e	e	e	e
Chemicals	—	—	—	—	—	—	—	—
Rubber	—	e	595	818	—	e	1427	2215

Source: Bureau of the Census, U.S. Dept. of Commerce, *County Business Patterns,* 1965, 1970, 1975, 1980.
[a] Number of employees for week including March 12.
[b] First quarter only in $ thousands.
[c] SIC 33 only.
[d] SIC 34 only.
[e] Withheld to avoid disclosing information for individual companies.

thermore, the textile industry, which dominated the county in 1965 with 63 percent of the manufacturing employment and 64 percent of the manufacturing payroll, represented only 42 percent of the manufacturing employment and 40 percent of the manufacturing payroll in 1980 (Table III-19). It should be noted, however, that much of the realignment in Randolph County has been into the furniture and apparel industries. Taken as a group, textiles, furniture, and apparel represented 79 percent of manufacturing employment in 1965 and 71 percent in 1980. This small decrease can be attributed to the growth in the rubber, metals, machinery, and electrical industries.

Rockingham County (Labor area: Reidsville-Eden, North Carolina)

Rockingham County appears to exemplify textile management's success in meeting the disparity of wages between textiles and high technology, high paying industry. Textiles, as Rockingham's leading industry, in 1965 represented 50 percent of the manufacturing employment and 49 percent of the manufacturing payroll (Table III-

TABLE III-20

Rockingham County, North Carolina
Manufacturing Employment and Payroll by Selected Industry
1965–1980

	Employment[a]				Payroll[b]			
	1965	1970	1975	1980	1965	1970	1975	1980
County	12,289	15,838	15,386	18,794	12,489	20,700	27,539	59,960
Furniture	e	e	—	500–999	e	e	—	e
Stone, Clay, & Glass	231	117	278	257	200	135	364	695
Metals	—	—	96[d]	482[d]	—	—	203[d]	2721[d]
Machinery	—	e	—	117	—	e	—	267
Electrical	—	e	—	100–249	—	e	—	e
Food	103	—	68	1000–2499	73	—	114	e
Textiles	6156	8972	9987	9178	6114	11,147	16,168	22,306
Apparel	2387	2639	1523	2467	2126	3385	2128	5888
Paper	—	—	—	—	—	—	—	—
Chemicals	—	—	—	—	—	—	—	—
Rubber	—	e	100–249	250–499	—	e	e	e

Source: Bureau of the Census, U.S. Dept. of Commerce, *County Business Patterns,* 1965, 1970, 1975, 1980.
[a] Number of employees for week including March 12.
[b] First quarter only in $ thousands.
[c] SIC 33 only.
[d] SIC 34 only.
[e] Withheld to avoid disclosing information for individual companies.

20). In 1980, textiles represented 49 percent of the manufacturing employment and 37 percent of the payroll for the county. In spite of a significant decline in its share of manufacturing payroll, textiles maintained its leadership in and share of the county's manufacturing employment.

Rockingham County appears to harbor significant growth opportunities with consistent growth in general population (Table III-5) and considerable investment in new capital expenditures (Table III-8). In fact, Rockingham County not only experienced a 404 percent increase in new capital expenditures for the period 1972 to 1977 (Table III-18), but in absolute terms it also led the counties presented in Table III-8 with new capital expenditures of $115.4 million in 1977. Fieldcrest is a principal textile employer in the Eden, North Carolina area.

Rutherford County (Labor area: Forest City-Rutherfordton, North Carolina)

Rutherford County has experienced very little in diversity and new capital expenditures (Table III-8). It has consistently ranked

TABLE III-21

Rutherford County, North Carolina
Manufacturing Employment and Payroll by Selected Industry
1965–1980

	Employment[a]				Payroll[b]			
	1965	1970	1975	1980	1965	1970	1975	1980
County	7924	9387	9171	11,555	7,555	11,970	16,312	31,145
Furniture	e	1122	1200	1584	e	1456	1835	3911
Stone, Clay, & Glass	—	—	—	50	—	—	—	63
Metals	—	—	—	—	—	—	—	—
Machinery	—	—	—	—	—	—	—	—
Electrical	—	—	—	20–99	—	—	—	e
Food	125	—	20–99	20–99	104	—	e	e
Textiles	6121	6783	5536	7348	6094	8833	10,293	20,718
Apparel	837	1133	1682	1290	684	1310	2761	2970
Paper	—	—	—	—	—	—	—	—
Chemicals	—	—	—	20–99	—	—	—	e
Rubber	—	—	416	736	—	—	758	1946

Source: Bureau of the Census, U.S. Dept. of Commerce, *County Business Patterns,* 1965, 1970,
        1975, 1980.
[a] Number of employees for week including March 12.
[b] First quarter only in $ thousands.
[c] SIC 33 only.
[d] SIC 34 only.
[e] Withheld to avoid disclosing information for individual companies.

in the bottom third with respect to absolute new capital expenditures and only recently experienced growth of 131 percent over 1972 to 1977 (Table III-9). The county's general population actually declined over the period 1950 to 1960 with modest increases since (Table III-5). Table III-21 shows that the textile industry has dominated manufacturing employment in the county, followed by furniture and apparel. The textile industry represented 77 percent of the manufacturing employment and 81 percent of the payroll in 1965 and still represented 64 percent and 67 percent respectively in 1980. Indeed, stone, clay, and glass; electrical; chemicals; and rubber combined accounted for less than 1,000 employees in 1980, and metals, machinery, and paper showed no representation. Additionally, it should be noted that in both 1965 and 1980 the textile industry's share of the county's manufacturing payroll exceeded its share of manufacturing employment. This is attributed to the significance of the lower paying furniture and apparel industries in manufacturing employment share, and the insignificance of new industry.

TABLE III-22

Stanly County, North Carolina
Manufacturing Employment and Payroll by Selected Industry
1965–1980

	Employment[a]				Payroll[b]			
	1965	1970	1975	1980	1965	1970	1975	1980
County	8669	11,144	8946	10,945	8151	13,830	15,432	28,646
Furniture	561	752	499	482	550	1006	935	1219
Stone, Clay, & Glass	150 [e]	159 [e]	105	154	138 [e]	176 [e]	205 [e]	393 [e]
Metals			500–999[c]	1000–2499[c]				
Machinery	—	—	—	—	—	[e]	[e]	[e]
Electrical	—	[e]	250–499	500–999	—			
Food	401	265	254	306	361	325	395	424
Textiles	5361	6936	5715	6796	4491	7901	8322	15,646
Apparel	1390	868	780	737	1530	784	1396	1277
Paper	—	—	—	—	—	—	—	—
Chemicals	—	—	—	—	—	—	—	[e]
Rubber	—	—	—	100–249	—	—	—	

Source: Bureau of the Census, U.S. Dept. of Commerce, *County Business Patterns*, 1965, 1970, 1975, 1980.
[a] Number of employees for week including March 12.
[b] First quarter only in $ thousands.
[c] SIC 33 only.
[d] SIC 34 only.
[e] Withheld to avoid disclosing information for individual companies.

Stanly County (Labor area: Albemarle, North Carolina)

Stanly County is one of only two counties presented (the other being Rockingham) which demonstrate stability in their textile labor force. Textiles accounted for 62 percent of the county's manufacturing employment in both 1965 and 1980 (Table III-22). However, in contrast to Rockingham County, textiles in Stanly County have also maintained a 55 percent share of manufacturing payroll for 1965 and 1980. This maintenance of payroll share is due to the small representation (less than 2,500 employees) of metals, electrical, and rubber industries, and no representation by machinery, chemicals, and paper. This pattern of slow diversification is further reinforced by noting the small expenditures on new capital (Table III-8) and the modest growth in general population (Table 3.5).

This examination of each of the twelve counties chosen for study in North Carolina has demonstrated the leadership of textiles, industrial realignment in some counties, with the stage set for realignment in others, evidence of textile labor force stability in two counties, and relative stagnation in two others.

TABLE III-23

South Carolina
General Population, State and Selected Counties
1950–1980

	1950	1960	Percent Change 1950–60	1970	Percent Change 1960–70	1980	Percent Change 1970–80
State	2,117,027	2,382,594	12.5	2,590,516	8.7	3,119,208	20.4
Anderson	90,664	98,478	8.6	105,474	7.1	133,235	26.3
Chester	32,597	30,888	−5.2	29,811	−3.5	30,148	1.1
Greenville	168,152	209,776	24.8	240,546	14.7	287,913	19.7
Lancaster	37,071	39,352	6.2	43,328	10.1	53,361	23.2
Laurens	46,974	47,609	1.4	49,713	4.4	52,214	5.0
Newberry	31,771	29,416	−7.4	29,273	−0.5	31,111	6.3
Oconee	39,050	40,224	0.3	40,728	1.3	48,611	19.4
Pickens	40,058	46,030	14.9	58,956	28.1	79,292	34.5
Spartanburg	150,349	156,830	4.3	173,724	10.8	201,553	16.0
York	71,596	78,760	10.0	85,216	8.2	106,720	25.2

Source: Bureau of the Census, U.S. Dept. of Commerce, 1980 *Census of Population and Housing—South Carolina;* 1950, 1960, 1970, *Census of Population Number of Inhabitants, U.S. Summary.*

THE SOUTH CAROLINA TEXTILE ENVIRONMENT

General population growth for South Carolina (20.4 percent, Table III-23) exceeded national growth (11.5 percent) for the period 1970 to 1980, and exceeded growth for North Carolina (15.6 percent) and Georgia (19.1 percent) over the same period. All of the ten counties presented for South Carolina experienced population growth, with Chester County showing the smallest growth at 1.1 percent and Pickens County showing the largest at 34.5 percent. Seven of the ten counties presented showed growth over 15 percent for the decade ending in 1980.[3]

With respect to manufacturing employment over a more recent period, 1972 to 1982, South Carolina experienced growth of 2 percent, with metals at 54 percent, machinery at 48 percent, and electrical at 63 percent leading the industries presented (Table III-24). As with North Carolina, textiles was the leading manufacturing employer in 1972 with 43.5 percent of the state's manufacturing employment, and remained the leading employer in 1982 with a 32.3 percent share (Table III-25). This leadership was sustained in spite of an absolute decline in textile employment from 154,000 in 1972 to 117,100 in 1982 (Table III-24).

Since the high technology industries are leading South Carolina's

[3] *Ibid.*

TABLE III-24

South Carolina

Manufacturing Employment by State and Selected Industries
1972–1982

	1972	1974	1976	1978	1980	1982	Percent Change 1972–1982
State	354,300	375,900	371,000	391,100	391,900	362,200	2
Furniture	4,900	4,700	4,500	5,000	4,800	4,600	−6
Stone, Clay, and Glass	11,000	12,300	10,800	11,700	10,900	10,200	−7
Metals[a]	8,700	10,800	11,700	14,000	14,300	13,400	54
Machinery	19,200	24,400	24,800	29,900	31,300	28,400	48
Electrical	13,000	18,100	15,900	19,500	22,000	21,200	63
Food	14,300	13,600	13,700	14,500	14,400	14,600	2
Textiles	154,000	155,500	149,500	143,400	136,900	117,100	−24
Apparel	45,500	44,300	46,200	48,300	46,400	44,900	−1
Paper	12,300	13,400	13,500	13,900	14,000	14,100	15
Chemicals	28,100	30,900	30,700	32,600	33,300	32,100	14
Rubber[b]	—	—	—	—	—	19,000	(6)

Source: U.S. Bureau of Labor Statistics, U.S. Dept. of Labor, *Employment and Earnings, States and Areas,* 1939–1982.
[a] SIC 34 only.
[b] Data not available for 1972–1980.

TABLE III-25

South Carolina

Selected Industry Percents of Total Manufacturing Employment
1972–1980

Industry	1972	1974	1976	1978	1980	1982
Furniture	1.4	1.2	1.2	1.3	1.2	1.3
Stone, Clay, and Glass	3.1	3.3	2.9	3.0	2.8	2.8
Metals[a]	2.5	2.9	3.2	3.6	3.6	3.7
Machinery	5.4	6.5	6.7	7.7	8.0	7.8
Electrical	3.7	4.8	4.3	4.9	5.6	5.8
Food	4.0	3.6	3.7	3.7	3.7	4.0
Textiles	43.5	41.4	40.3	36.8	34.9	32.3
Apparel	12.9	11.8	12.4	12.3	11.8	12.4
Paper	3.5	3.6	3.6	3.5	3.6	3.9
Chemicals	7.9	8.2	8.3	8.3	8.5	8.9
Rubber[b]	—	—	—	—	—	5.2

Source: Derived from Table III-27.
[a] SIC 34 only.
[b] Data not available for 1972–1980.

TABLE III-26

South Carolina

New Capital Expenditures by State and Selected Counties

(in millions)

1963–1982

State	1963	1967	Percent Change 1963-67	1972	Percent Change 1967-72	1977	Percent Change 1972-77	1982	Percent Change 1977-82
State	$ 179.3	$ 416.6	132.3	$ 506.9	21.7	$ 788.6	55.6	$ 1502.5	90.5
Anderson	7.9	60.6	667.1	23.4	-61.4	46.1	97.0	66.7	44.7
Chester	a	4.4	—	2.9	-34.1	6.2	113.8	31.4	406.0
Greenville	15.2	49.4	225.0	63.3	28.1	120.2	89.9	195.4	62.6
Lancaster	a	a	—	a	—	3.1	—	16.1	419.0
Laurens	6.1	14.6	139.3	4.9	-66.4	12.0	144.9	16.5	37.5
Newberry	1.0	3.6	260.0	4.8	33.3	4.7	2.1	18.0	283.0
Oconee	3.9	5.5	41.0	3.8	-30.9	4.3	13.2	15.2	253.5
Pickens	5.7	5.3	-7.0	20.8	292.5	39.1	88.0	48.2	232.7
Spartanburg	13.5	57.9	328.9	110.6	91.0	52.7	-52.4	107.9	104.7
York	4.8	9.1	89.6	17.5	92.3	36.1	106.3	82.4	128.2

Source: Bureau of the Census, U.S. Dept. of Commerce, *Census of Manufactures*, 1963, 1967, 1977, 1982.
Note: ᵃ=Withheld to avoid disclosing information for individual companies.

TABLE III-27

South Carolina
*State and Selected Industry Average Hourly Earnings for Production
Workers
1972–1982*

	1972	1974	1976	1978	1980	1982	Percent Change 1972–1982
State Average	$ 2.80	$ 3.32	$ 3.91	$ 4.66	$ 5.59	$ 6.68	139
Furniture	2.54	2.76	3.28	3.94	4.86	5.39	112
Stone, Clay, and Glass	3.24	3.75	4.45	5.26	6.14	7.48	131
Metals[a]	2.84	3.38	3.97	4.59	5.55	6.41	126
Machinery	3.08	3.66	4.35	5.07	6.18	7.34	138
Electrical	2.59	3.06	3.66	4.35	.5.24	6.16	138
Food	2.47	2.87	3.48	4.16	4.92	5.88	138
Textiles	2.74	3.22	3.77	4.46	5.25	6.08	122
Apparel	2.09	2.53	2.93	3.50	4.13	4.67	123
Paper	4.35	4.88	5.58	6.79	8.28	9.76	124
Chemicals	3.81	4.36	5.31	6.31	7.69	9.26	143
Rubber[b]	—	—	—	—	—	—	—

Source: U.S. Bureau of Labor Statistics, U.S. Dept. of Labor, *Employment and Earnings, States and Areas,* 1939–1982.
[a] SIC 34 only.
[b] Data not available.

growth, the state has also experienced consistent growth in new capital expenditures over the period 1963 to 1982 (Table III-26). South Carolina's absolute new capital expenditure, however, has remained below the levels of new capital expenditures occurring in both North Carolina and Georgia. In 1982, $1,502.5 million was spent in South Carolina in contrast to $2,588.6 million in North Carolina and $1,921.7 million in Georgia. Although South Carolina is experiencing some industrial realignment, the state's diversification is progressing more slowly than North Carolina and Georgia. One explanation for this slower growth is apparent upon comparing wage differentials for the three states. Tables III-9, III-27, and III-42 show average hourly earnings for production workers in selected industries for the three states. An examination of these tables points out that South Carolina textile workers are paid the highest and South Carolina metals, machinery, and electrical workers are paid the lowest among the three states. Therefore, the wage disparity, which is providing an impetus to industrial realignment in North Carolina and Georgia, is not prevalent in South Carolina.

With respect to race distribution, Table III-10 shows that the race

TABLE III-28

Anderson County, South Carolina
Manufacturing Employment and Payroll by Selected Industry
1965–1980

	Employment[a]				Payroll[b]			
	1965	1970	1975	1980	1965	1970	1975	1980
County	17,951	26,394	21,079	24,531	19,107	29,030	35,293	75,299
Furniture	—	—	—	—	—	—	—	—
Stone, Clay, & Glass	e	e	1000–2499	1000–2499	e	e	e	e
Metals	—	137[d]	122[d]	675[d]	—	156[d]	231[d]	1966[d]
Machinery	258	526	526	832	300	726	1171	2861
Electrical	e	e	1000–2499	1000–2499	e	e	e	e
Food	460	569	478	329	473	685	1158	1290
Textiles	12,195	12,445	11,938	12,498	13,288	17,265	18,572	36,952
Apparel	1815	2275	2474	2503	1284	1938	2731	4613
Paper	—	—	20–99	—	—	—	e	—
Chemicals	101	e	1000–2499	101	e	e	e	e
Rubber	—	—	428	1000–2499	—	—	1123	e

Source: Bureau of the Census, U.S. Dept. of Commerce, *County Business Patterns,* 1965, 1970,
    1975, 1980.
[a] Number of employees for week including March 12.
[b] First quarter only in $ thousands.
[c] SIC 33 only.
[d] SIC 34 only.
[e] Withheld to avoid disclosing information for individual companies.

realignment suggested for the South as a region is also evident in
South Carolina. In 1950, 38.9 percent of the state's population was
non-white. By 1980, this representation had fallen 7.7 percentage
points to 31.2 percent. Although South Carolina showed the most
change, it is still the most racially balanced of the three states with
one out of three individuals classified as non-white as opposed to
North Carolina and Georgia with closer to one out of four individuals
classified as non-white in 1980.

SOUTH CAROLINA COUNTY PROFILES

With the characteristics of South Carolina as a state in the background, the following section provides population, manufacturing
employment and payroll, and new capital expenditures data for
each of ten counties within the state.

Anderson County (Labor area: Anderson, South Carolina)

Anderson County has experienced consistent growth in its general
population since 1950, but only recently has this growth exceeded

TABLE III-29

Chester County, South Carolina
Manufacturing Employment and Payroll by Selected Industry
1965–1980

	Employment[a]				Payroll[b]			
	1965	1970	1975	1980	1965	1970	1975	1980
County	5175	6138	6666	8184	5240	8343	9991	22,730
Furniture	—	—	—	—	—	—	—	—
Stone, Clay, & Glass	—	—	—	100–249	—	—	—	e
Metals	—	—	177ᵈ	248ᵈ	—	—	149ᵈ	594ᵈ
Machinery	e	e	100–249	100–249	e	e	e	e
Electrical	—	—	—	—	—	—	—	—
Food	—	—	100–249	100–249	—	—	e	e
Textiles	4450	4907	2500–4999	5000–9999	4570	6892	e	e
Apparel	e	734	956	1549	e	727	1392	3508
Paper	—	—	—	—	—	—	—	—
Chemicals	—	—	100–249	100–249	—	—	e	e
Rubber	—	—	—	—	—	—	—	—

Source: Bureau of the Census, U.S. Dept. of Commerce, *County Business Patterns,* 1965, 1970, 1975, 1980.

a Number of employees for week including March 12.
b First quarter only in $ thousands.
c SIC 33 only.
d SIC 34 only.
e Withheld to avoid disclosing information for individual companies.

state levels (Table III-23). Furthermore, Table III-28 shows that the county's manufacturing employment has also increased from 17,951 in 1965 to 24,531 in 1980 for an increase of 36.7 percent. This increase is generally accounted for by the establishment and recent growth of the metals, machinery, electrical, chemicals, and rubber industries. Although textiles was, and still is, the county's leading manufacturing employer, its growth over the 1965 to 1980 period was only 2.5 percent. In 1965, textiles accounted for 68 percent of the county's manufacturing employment and 70 percent of its manufacturing payroll. By 1980, this representation had fallen to 51 percent and 49 percent, respectively. Although South Carolina, on average, demonstrates a measure of stability and resistance to significant realignment, it appears that Anderson County may soon be well diversified into high technology, high wage paying industry.

Chester County (Labor area: Chester, South Carolina)

Although the metals, machinery, and chemicals industries have recently located on a small scale in Chester County, textiles is still the county's leading manufacturing employer followed by apparel

TABLE III-30

Greenville County, South Carolina
Manufacturing Employment and Payroll by Selected Industry
1965-1980

	Employment[a]				Payroll[b]			
	1965	1970	1975	1980	1965	1970	1975	1980
County	37,337	44,047	46,067	53,870	39,666	63,015	93,838	177,520
Furniture	310	572	505	785	322	813	1014	2147
Stone, Clay, & Glass	411	428	373	516	464	679	1024	1667
Metals	331[d]	956	1064	1999	373[d]	1361	2863	6430
Machinery	2557	4175	6113	7651	3250	7370	15,653[e]	27,658[e]
Electrical	898	1688	2500–4999	2500–4999	897	2533		
Food	1497	1808	1465	1516	1426	2476	3281	4503
Textiles	19,913	18,482	17,546	15,041	22,509	25,590	28,031	44,684
Apparel	7843	7638	4980	5198	6081	7700	6015	10,213
Paper	1064	1375	1719	2465	1252	2295	4641	8394
Chemicals	745	e	3207	3672	1077	e	6398	13,419
Rubber	—	673	1886	4861	—	1195	5460	22,667

Source: Bureau of the Census, U.S. Dept. of Commerce, *County Business Patterns*, 1965, 1970, 1975, 1980.
[a] Number of employees for week including March 12.
[b] First quarter only in $ thousands.
[c] SIC 33 only.
[d] SIC 34 only.
[e] Withheld to avoid disclosing information for individual companies.

(Table III-29). It appears that this dominance and concentration will persist as several industries are as yet unrepresented in the county. Furthermore, general population in the county fell over the period 1950 to 1970 and grew a slight 1.1 percent in the decade ending in 1980 (Table III-23). In terms of new capital expenditures (Table III-26), Chester County has consistently ranked near the bottom of the counties studied except for the period 1977–82 when considerable investments were made. This county has yet to experience significant industrial realignment, although such realignment may occur through spillover for neighboring York County.

Greenville County (Labor area: Greenville-Spartanburg, South Carolina)

Greenville County is one of two counties (the other is neighboring Spartanburg County) presenting which shows comparatively mature diversification as of 1980 (Table III-30). With consistent increases in general population, with growth and leadership in new capital expenditures (195.4 million in 1982, Table III-26), and with an increase in manufacturing employment of 44.3 percent over the

TABLE III-31

Lancaster County, South Carolina
Manufacturing Employment and Payroll by Selected Industry
1965–1980

	Employment[a]				Payroll[b]			
	1965	1970	1975	1980	1965	1970	1975	1980
County	9767	10,179	9187	11,724	10,410	13,855	14,268	32,374
Furniture	—	—	—	—	—	e	—	—
Stone, Clay, & Glass	e	e	100–249	100–249	e		e	e
Metals	—	—	100–249[d]	100–249[d]	—	—	e	e
Machinery	e	268	279	357	e	443	589	1243
Electrical	e	e	250–499	1000–2499	e	e	e	e
Food	e	—	—	20–99	e	—	—	e
Textiles	7559	10,179	5000–9999	5000–9999	7725	13,855	e	e
Apparel	e	e	250–499	500–999	e	e	e	e
Paper	—	—	—	—	—	—	—	—
Chemicals	—	—	—	—	—	—	—	—
Rubber	—	—	—	—	—	—	—	—

Source: Bureau of the Census, U.S. Dept. of Commerce, *County Business Patterns,* 1965, 1970, 1975, 1980.
[a] Number of employees for week including March 12.
[b] First quarter only in $ thousands.
[c] SIC 33 only.
[d] SIC 34 only.
[e] Withheld to avoid disclosing information for individual companies.

period 1965 to 1980, Greenville County is experiencing industrial realignment and general prosperity. This prosperity, however, has been at the expense of textile employment which fell 24.5 percent over the period 1965 to 1980. In 1965, the textile industry accounted for 53 percent of the county's manufacturing employment and 57 percent of its manufacturing payroll. By 1980, this representation had fallen to 28 percent and 25 percent, respectively. With high technology industries showing significant growth in the county, textile management is faced with a challenge to compete in the county's labor market. With textiles and apparel both showing absolute declines in employment in the county, they are evidently faring poorly in this competition.

Lancaster County (Labor area: Lancaster, South Carolina)

Table III-31 shows that Lancaster County is another South Carolina county lacking significant diversification. The textile industry is the dominant manufacturing employer in the county, with the electrical industry second. Although much data are withheld on county employment, payroll, and new capital expenditures to avoid

TABLE III-32

Laurens County, South Carolina
Manufacturing Employment and Payroll by Selected Industry
1965–1980

	Employment[a]				Payroll[b]			
	1965	1970	1975	1980	1965	1970	1975	1980
County	8048	9287	8233	9922	8576	12,758	14,923	28,391
Furniture	—	—	—	—	—	—	—	—
Stone, Clay, & Glass	e	e	1000–2499	1000–2499	e	e	e	e
Metals	—	—	250–499[d]	500–999[d]	—	—	e	e
Machinery	e	e	1000–2499	1000–2499	e	e	e	e
Electrical	—	—	—	—	—	—	—	—
Food	—	—	—	100–249	—	—	—	e
Textiles	4832	5108	4194	4961	5401	6987	6317	14,036
Apparel	e	583	675	806	e	506	757[e]	1292[e]
Paper	—	—	20–99	20–99	—	—	e	—
Chemicals	—	—	—	—	—	—	—	—
Rubber	—	—	—	—	—	—	—	—

Source: Bureau of the Census, U.S. Dept. of Commerce, *County Business Patterns*, 1965, 1970, 1975, 1980.
[a] Number of employees for week including March 12.
[b] First quarter only in $ thousands.
[c] SIC 33 only.
[d] SIC 34 only.
[e] Withheld to avoid disclosing information for individual companies.

disclosing information on individual companies, it is at least qualitatively apparent that the county is undiversified, and those industries established in the county are only represented by a small number of employers. Lancaster County parallels the state's generally slow industrial realignment and basically secure and stable labor market.

Laurens County (Labor area: Laurens-Clinton, South Carolina)

The textile industry is the leading employer in Laurens County accounting for 50 percent of the county's manufacturing employment and 49 percent of its manufacturing payroll in 1980. This representation, however, was down from 1965 shares of 60 percent and 63 percent, respectively (Table III-32). With general population growing consistently, albeit slowly, and new capital expenditures seesawing, Laurens County also reflects the state's general dormancy. Although the county does show a small representation in metals and machinery, it is lacking any representation from the electrical, chemical, or rubber industries and has an insignificant

TABLE III-33

Newberry County, South Carolina
Manufacturing Employment and Payroll by Selected Industry
1965–1980

	Employment[a]				Payroll[b]			
	1965	1970	1975	1980	1965	1970	1975	1980
County	3665	4451	4721	5895	3452	5649	7248	16,333
Furniture	—	—	—	—	—	—	—	—
Stone, Clay, & Glass	—	e	—	—	—	e	—	—
Metals	—	—	—	—	—	—	—	—
Machinery	—	—	—	—	—	—	—	—
Electrical	—	—	100–249	100–249	—	—	e	e
Food	133	291	250–499	1000–2499	128	339	e	e
Textiles	2354	2710[e]	2358	2421	2547	3734[e]	3503	6746[e]
Apparel	537	e	601	500–999	412	e	903	e
Paper	—	e	20–99	100–249	—	e	e	e
Chemicals	—	—	—	—	—	—	—	—
Rubber	—	—	—	—	—	—	—	—

Source: Bureau of the Census, U.S. Dept. of Commerce, *County Business Patterns*, 1965, 1970, 1975, 1980.
[a] Number of employees for week including March 12.
[b] First quarter only in $ thousands.
[c] SIC 33 only.
[d] SIC 34 only.
[e] Withheld to avoid disclosing information for individual companies.

presence in the paper industry. It will be interesting to note in the future if Laurens County will explode like Anderson County, both of which are neighbors of well diversified Greenville County.

Newberry County (Labor area: Newberry, South Carolina)

In 1976, the only significant manufacturing industries in Newberry County were food, textiles, and apparel, accounting respectively for 4 percent, 64 percent, and 15 percent of the county's manufacturing employment and 4 percent, 73 percent, and 12 percent of the county's manufacturing payroll (Table III-33). Fifteen years later only two new industries had located in the county. These industries were paper and electrical, each with fewer than 250 employees. With general population having decreased over the period 1950 to 1970, and only recently increased by 6.3 percent over 1970 to 1980, and with new capital expenditures averaging some of the lowest in South Carolina, Newberry County remains one of the least economically developed counties studied, and it is very unlikely that this situation will change significantly in the near future.

TABLE III-34

Oconee County, South Carolina
Manufacturing Employment and Payroll by Selected Industry
1965–1980

	Employment[a]				Payroll[b]			
	1965	1970	1975	1980	1965	1970	1975	1980
County	8731	7288	5796	7632	8341	9002	8861	17,668
Furniture	—	—	—	—	—	—	—	—
Stone, Clay, & Glass	—	—	—	—	—	—	—	—
Metals	—	—	—	20–99[d]	—	—	—	e
Machinery	162	254 e	—	133	172	408 e	—	362
Electrical	—	—	—	—	—	—	—	—
Food	122	—	—	—	69	—	—	—
Textiles	5105	2546 e	1890	2052	5441	3277 e	2800	5089
Apparel	1482	—	1643	2146	1019	—	1961	3941
Paper	—	e	—	—	—	e	—	—
Chemicals	—	—	—	—	—	—	e	e
Rubber	—	—	100–249	100–249	—	—	—	—

Source: Bureau of the Census, U.S. Dept. of Commerce, *County Business Patterns,* 1965, 1970, 1975, 1980.
[a] Number of employees for week including March 12.
[b] First quarter only in $ thousands.
[c] SIC 33 only.
[d] SIC 34 only.
[e] Withheld to avoid disclosing information for individual companies.

Oconee County (Labor area: Seneca, South Carolina)

Oconee County rivals previously discussed Chester, Lancaster, and Newberry Counties for the least investment in new capital expenditures. Except for a recent surge in general population, the county has also grown slowly over the last 30 years. In fact, over the period 1965 to 1980, manufacturing employment fell in the county by 12.6 percent from 8,371 to 7,632 with the textile industry contributing the most to this decline with a reduction in its employment by 59.8 percent (Table III-34). Other manufacturing industries which lost employees during this period were machinery, electrical, food, and chemicals; only metals, apparel, and rubber showed increases. Oconee is another South Carolina county with an unpredictable economic future.

Pickens County (Labor area: Greenville-Spartanburg, South Carolina)

Although only six of the eleven industries shown in Table III-35 are actually established in Pickens County, the county is faring quite well economically. General population and new capital ex-

TABLE III-35

Pickens County, South Carolina
Manufacturing Employment and Payroll by Selected Industry
1965–1980

	Employment[a]				Payroll[b]			
	1965	1970	1975	1980	1965	1970	1975	1980
County	11,057	13,672	13,415	17,289	11,442	18,536	20,854	47,692
Furniture	—	—	—	—	—	—	—	—
Stone, Clay, & Glass	—	—	—	—	—	—	—	—
Metals	—	e	350–748	91[d]	—	e	e	285[d]
Machinery	e	e	1518	4540	e	e	2942	13,000
Electrical	e	—	500–999	e	—	—	e	e
Food	—	—	—	—	—	—	—	—
Textiles	4777	7188	8445	8517	4918	9713	12,442	23,933
Apparel	923	1286	1013	837	849	1426	1429	1787
Paper	—	e	—	—	—	e	—	—
Chemicals	—	—	—	—	—	—	—	e
Rubber	—	—	—	250–499	—	—	—	—

Source: Bureau of the Census, U.S. Dept. of Commerce, *County Business Patterns*, 1965, 1970, 1975, 1980.
[a] Number of employees for week including March 12.
[b] First quarter only in $ thousands.
[c] SIC 33 only.
[d] SIC 34 only.
[e] Withheld to avoid disclosing information for individual companies.

penditures have shown excellent growth as has manufacturing employment which grew 56.4 percent over the period 1965 to 1980. Only one industry, apparel, showed a decline for the period at 9.3 percent with textiles and machinery both showing strong gains. Indeed, atypical of South Carolina counties, the textile industry in Pickens County increased its share of manufacturing employment from 43 percent in 1965 to 49 percent in 1980, and its share of manufacturing payroll from 43 percent in 1965 to 50 percent in 1980. In addition, with strong representations in the county by the metals and electrical industries, and a minor presence in rubber, the county is primed for significant diversification and industrial realignment. And, as with Anderson County, this industrial realignment may result from neighboring Greenville County's spillover.

Spartanburg County (Labor area: Greenville-Spartanburg, South Carolina)

Spartanburg County is one of two South Carolina counties which has shown comparatively mature diversification (Table III-36). Like neighboring Greenville County, Spartanburg shows consistent

TABLE III-36

Spartanburg County, South Carolina
Manufacturing Employment and Payroll by Selected Industry
1965–1980

	Employment[a]				Payroll[b]			
	1965	1970	1975	1980	1965	1970	1975	1980
County	29,693	33,987	35,352	40,267	31,510	49,870	73,590	133,980
Furniture	e	e	—	95	e	e	—	92
Stone, Clay, & Glass	e	927	1174	1252	e	1325	2567	4111
Metals	e	954[d]	2155	2244	e	1364	5101	8145
Machinery	1161	1048	1032	2590	1306	1749	2046	9318
Electrical	—	572	100–249	485	—	863	e	1329
Food	672	810	873	1039	742	1021	1617	2921
Textiles	20,151	17,110	14,187	16,376	21,663	25,040	22,404	49,048
Apparel	3203	6176	5513	5048	2456	7027	8389	12,649
Paper	551	787	892	995	574	1168	2125	3342
Chemicals	405	1583	3668	3368	414	3000	10,916	15,202
Rubber	—	442	711	2171	—	565	1579	8757

Source: Bureau of the Census, U.S. Dept. of Commerce, *County Business Patterns,* 1965, 1970, 1975, 1980.
[a] Number of employees for week including March 12.
[b] First quarter only in $ thousands.
[c] SIC 33 only.
[d] SIC 34 only.
[e] Withheld to avoid disclosing information for individual companies.

growth in general population and manufacturing employment (35.6 percent over the period 1965 to 1980, Table III-36), leadership in new capital expenditures, and tremendous growth in high technology, high paying industry. Also consistent with Greenville County, the textile industry has fared poorly during this period of growth, showing a decline in employment of 18.7 percent. In 1965, textiles accounted for 68 percent of the county's manufacturing employment and 69 percent of its manufacturing payroll. By 1980, this representation had fallen to 41 percent and 37 percent, respectively. Spartanburg County exhibits the industrial realignment which is occurring in the South, although South Carolina on average is only primed for that realignment.

York County (Labor area: Rock Hill, South Carolina)

York County shows consistent growth in general population for the period 1950 to 1980 with recent growth exceeding the state's level. The county has also shown tremendous growth in new capital expenditures although it has never ranked high among the counties presented. This growth in new capital expenditures is indicative of

TABLE III-37

York County, South Carolina
Manufacturing Employment and Payroll by Selected Industry
1965–1980

	Employment[a]				Payroll[b]			
	1965	1970	1975	1980	1965	1970	1975	1980
County	14,631	16,011	12,849	15,684	16,728	23,421	25,596	50,230
Furniture	—	—	—	—	—	—	—	—
Stone, Clay, & Glass	—	—	83	246	—	—	115[e]	750
Metals	—	—	120–348	322[d]	—	—	—	1112[d]
Machinery	[e]	127	139	187	[e]	203	371	576
Electrical	—	—	—	—	—	—	—	—
Food	282	174	113	78	220	216	218	177
Textiles	10,095	8760	7672	8507	10,866	11,717	13,034	23,207
Apparel	[e]	432	620	898	[e]	364	815	1796
Paper	[e]	[e]	1000–2499	1000–2499	[e]	[e]	[e]	[e]
Chemicals	[e]	[e]	1000–2499	1000–2499	[e]	[e]	[e]	[e]
Rubber	—	[e]	100–249	406	—	[e]	[e]	1119

Source: Bureau of the Census, U.S. Dept. of Commerce, *County Business Patterns,* 1965, 1970, 1975, 1980.
[a] Number of employees for week including March 12.
[b] First quarter only in $ thousands.
[c] SIC 33 only.
[d] SIC 34 only.
[e] Withheld to avoid disclosing information for individual companies.

the diversification and realignment that industry in the county is presently experiencing. Indeed, all of the high technology, high paying industries with the exception of electrical, show significant presence in the county as of 1980. This diversification has occurred to the detriment of textiles, which dominated manufacturing employment and payroll in the county in 1965 (Table III-37). By 1980, textiles accounted for only 54 percent of the county's manufacturing employment and 46 percent of its manufacturing payroll. Interestingly, although the textile industry represents a significantly smaller share of the manufacturing employment, payroll share has declined minimally. In meeting the effects of diversification on the labor market, it appears that textile management in the county has raised wages substantially to retain employees.

Although several of the South Carolina counties presented are comparatively well diversified, or primed for future diversification, in aggregate the state is realigning slowly among manufacturing industries. This appears, in some cases, to be the result of higher textile wages. Indeed, South Carolina's textile earnings surpass

TABLE III-38

Georgia
General Population, State and Selected Counties
1950–1980

	1950	1960	Percent Change 1950–60	1970	Percent Change 1960–70	1980	Percent Change 1970–80
State	3,444,578	3,943,116	14.5	4,589,575	16.4	5,464,265	19.1
Floyd	62,899	69,130	9.9	73,742	6.7	79,800	8.2
Muscogee	118,028	158,623	34.4	167,377	5.5	170,108	1.6
Troup	49,841	47,189	−5.3	44,466	−5.8	50,003	12.4
Whitfield	34,432	42,109	22.2	55,108	30.9	65,780	19.4

Source: Bureau of the Census, U.S. Dept. of Commerce, *1980 Census of Population and Housing—Georgia;* 1950, 1960, 1970, *Census of Population, Number of Inhabitants, U.S. Summary.*

those of North Carolina and Georgia and compete favorably with newer industry.

THE GEORGIA TEXTILE ENVIRONMENT

The general population for Georgia has grown consistently since 1950 with faster growth occurring more recently (Table III-38). Georgia's growth of 16.4 percent from 1960 to 1970 and 19.1 percent from 1970 to 1980 exceeded national rates of 13.3 percent and 11.5 percent, respectively.[4] Over the period 1950 to 1980, Georgia's 58.6 percent growth in general population also exceeded North Carolina's growth of 44.6 percent and South Carolina's growth of 47.3 percent. In contrast to the state's general population growth trend, three of the four counties presented in Table III-38 showed their strongest growth prior to 1970. The exception shown is Troup County, which lost population prior to 1970 and showed growth of 12.4 percent for the period 1970 to 1980.

With respect to manufacturing employment over a more recent period 1972 to 1982, Georgia experienced growth of 5.0 percent, with the major labor intensive industries—furniture, textiles, and apparel—declining. (Table III-39). Metals, machinery, and electrical employment grew the fastest with growth rates over 45 percent. In spite of the growth by high technology industries, textiles and apparel lost very little share in the state's manufacturing employment (Table III-40).

[4] *Ibid.*

TABLE III-39

Georgia
Manufacturing Employment for State and Selected Industry
1972–1982

	1972	1974	1976	1978	1980	1982	Percent Change 1972–82
State	476,600	483,700	476,300	515,800	519,200	500,900	5
Furniture	10,800	9,700	8,300	9,800	9,400	9,400	−13
Stone, Clay, & Glass	15,600	17,000	15,300	18,000	17,700	16,000	3
Metals	11,000	12,800	12,900	15,500	16,500	16,100	46
Machinery	13,900	16,900	16,800	19,800	22,300	20,700	49
Electrical	13,400	16,100	14,800	18,300	20,300	23,100	80
Food	53,000	53,300	53,100	56,400	59,300	58,500	10
Textiles	119,500	123,400	121,100	123,700	117,600	104,200	−13
Apparel	73,300	71,500	72,700	74,500	72,300	69,500	−5
Paper	24,600	26,300	25,500	27,300	28,400	27,500	12
Chemicals	14,400	15,900	15,600	16,100	16,900	17,100	19

Source U.S. Bureau of Labor Statistics, U.S. Dept. of Labor, *Employment and Earnings, States and Areas*, 1939–1982.

Expenditures on new capital in each of the three counties studied have been considerable over the period 1963–1982, however, a slight decrease in expenditures was experienced in Troup and Whitfield Counties between 1977 and 1982. Table III-41 also shows that new

TABLE III-40

Georgia
Selected Industry Percents of Total Manufacturing Employment
1972–1982

Industry	1972	1974	1976	1978	1980	1982
Furniture	2.3	2.0	1.7	1.8	1.8	1.9
Stone, Clay, & Glass	3.3	3.5	3.2	3.5	3.4	3.2
Metals	2.3	2.6	2.7	3.0	3.2	3.2
Machinery	2.9	3.5	3.5	3.8	4.3	4.1
Electrical	2.8	3.3	3.1	3.5	3.9	4.6
Food	11.1	11.0	11.1	10.9	11.4	11.7
Textiles	25.1	25.5	25.4	24.0	22.6	21.0
Apparel	15.4	14.8	15.3	14.4	13.9	13.9
Paper	5.1	5.4	5.4	5.3	5.5	5.5
Chemicals	3.0	3.3	3.3	3.1	3.2	3.4

Source: Derived from Table III-44

TABLE III-41

Georgia

New Capital Expenditures by State and Selected Counties

1963–1982

(in millions)

	1963	1967	Percent Change 1963–67	1972	Percent Change 1967–72	1977	Percent Change 1972–77	1982	Percent Change 1977–82
State	$ 202.2	$ 423.3	109.3	$ 688.3	62.6	$ 1,143.4	66.1	$ 1921.7	68.0
Floyd	5.3[a]	14.9[a]	181.1	15.6	4.7	32.0	105.1	35.4	10.6
Muscogee								67.7	—
Troup	2.0	6.0	200.0	9.0	50.0	19.5	116.7	19.4	−0.5
Whitfield	4.1	8.7	112.2	23.8	173.6	40.3	69.3	39.2	−2.8

Source: Bureau of the Census, U.S. Dept. of Commerce, *Census of Manufactures,* 1963, 1967, 1977, 1982.
Note: [a] = Withheld to avoid disclosing information for individual companies.

TABLE III-42

Georgia
Average Hourly Earnings for Production Workers
by State and Selected Industry
1972–1982

	1972	1974	1976	1978	1980	1982	Percent Change 1972–1982
State Average	$ 3.04	$ 3.50	$ 4.10	$ 4.88	$ 5.77	$ 6.75	122
Furniture	2.58	2.95	3.43	4.45	4.39	5.04	95
Stone, Clay, & Glass	3.25	3.75	4.33	5.10	6.24	7.47	130
Metals	3.74	4.50	5.36	6.33	7.43	8.72	133
Machinery	3.39	4.18	4.20	5.55	6.82	7.17	112
Electrical	3.73	4.00	4.58	5.50	6.51	7.49	100
Food	2.89	3.34	3.92	4.71	5.30	6.24	116
Textiles	2.71	3.17	3.62	4.17	5.02	5.82	115
Apparel	2.24	2.58	2.92	3.47	4.03	4.60	105
Paper	4.20	4.79	5.87	6.99	8.35	10.11	141
Chemicals	3.40	4.04	4.74	5.87	6.71	8.21	141

Source U.S. Bureau of Labor Statistics, U.S. Dept. of Labor, *Employment and Earnings, States and Areas,* 1939–1982.

capital expenditures in the state have grown consistently over the period 1963 to 1982. This growth from $202.2 million in 1963 to $1,921.7 million in 1982 was faster than that found in South Carolina and North Carolina. Since textiles and apparel have not lost significant shares in manufacturing employment, it appears that growth in new capital expenditures for the state includes growth in expenditures for the textile industry. In contrast to South Carolina, which apparently has maintained textile labor stability partially through wage increases, Georgia apparently is competing with new industry through rapid modernization. The fact remains, however, that widespread modernization has occurred throughout the textile industry in North Carolina, South Carolina, and Georgia.

Table III-42 provides evidence on the textile industry's relative wage position in Georgia. Over the period 1972 to 1978, only the electrical, furniture, machinery, and apparel industries experienced slower growth in average hourly earnings for production workers than textiles. Additionally, only apparel paid wages lower than textiles among the manufacturing industries in the state. Therefore, textile management in Georgia is not responding to a competitive labor market with comparable wages, but with other mechanisms to reduce the labor force through modernization.

With respect to race distribution in Georgia, Table III-10 shows that in 1950 whites represented 69.1 percent of the state's population versus 72.3 percent in 1980. This realignment is consistent with that occurring in the South generally as well as in North Carolina and South Carolina. Georgia holds the median in racial balance among the three states being considered.

GEORGIA COUNTY PROFILES

The characteristics of Georgia as a state, as presented above, provide background for a study of Tables III-43 through III-46 as well as earlier Tables III-38, III-39, III-40, and III-41, which provide population, manufacturing employment and payroll, and new expenditures data for each of four counties within the state. A brief examination of these data for each county follows.

Floyd County (Labor area: Rome, Georgia)

Floyd County has experienced consistent growth in general population since 1950 (Table III-38) and consistent growth in new capital expenditures for the period 1965 to 1982 (Table III-41). The county is somewhat diversified with representatives from the metals, electrical, food, textiles, and apparel industries. Textiles increased its share of manufacturing employment in the county between 1965 and 1980, while other industries appeared to remain stable or to decline (Table III-43). Floyd County's realignment, therefore, is not consistent with Georgia or the South. Furthermore, although textile's share of employment has risen, its share of manufacturing payroll declined from 1965 to 1980. The textile industry grew in spite of wage disparity with high technology industries.

Muscogee County (Labor area: Columbus, Georgia)

In contrast with the general growth of textiles in Georgia, the textile industry in Muscogee has declined in employment from 9,653 in 1965 to 7,342 in 1980 for a net change of −23.9 percent (Table III-44). In 1965, textiles accounted for 59 percent of its manufacturing payroll. By 1980, this representation had fallen to 40 percent and 38 percent, respectively. The industries which have contributed significantly to the county's 13.4 percent rise in manufacturing employment have included metals, machinery, electrical, food, and rubber. Lesser growth has occurred in stone, clay, and glass; paper; and chemicals. Therefore, Muscogee County is experiencing industrial realignment consistent with that of the South with increasing diversification into high technology, high paying industry.

Employee Relations in the Textile Industry

TABLE III-43

Floyd County, Georgia
Manufacturing Employment and Payroll by Selected Industry
1965–1980

	Employment[a]				Payroll[b]			
	1965	1970	1975	1980	1965	1970	1975	1980
County	11,109	12,168	12,141	13,758	13,563	18,577	27,576	47,428
Furniture	e	e	250–499	500–999	e	e	e	e
Stone, Clay, & Glass	—	—	60	65	—	—	102	176
Metals	e	145[c]	782[c]	600–1248	e	170	1770	e
Machinery	218	130	118	201	248	172	223	567
Electrical	e	e	1000–2499	1000–2499	e	e	e	e
Food	848	827	753	983	875	1275	1715	3520
Textiles	4177	5066	5861	6347	4826	7247	10,388	18,827
Apparel	814	869	415	504	598	791	695	1042
Paper	e	e	500–999	1000–2499	e	e	e	e
Chemicals	e	e	250–499		e	e	e	e
Rubber	—	—	—	20–99	—	—	—	e

Source: Bureau of the Census, U.S. Dept. of Commerce, *County Business Patterns,* 1965, 1970, 1975, 1980.
[a] Number of employees for week including March 12.
[b] First quarter only in $ thousands.
[c] SIC 33 only.
[d] SIC 34 only.
[e] Withheld to avoid disclosing information for individual companies.

Troup County (Labor area: La Grange, Georgia)

Besides being located in the southwest corner of Georgia, Troup and Muscogee Counties also share industrial realignment and diversification trends. These trends include a reduction in textile employment and the establishment of new high technology industries. In Troup County, textile employment has fallen from 5,712 in 1965 to 4,348 in 1980 for a net change of −23.9 percent (Table III-45). Textile's share in the county's manufacturing employment and payroll has fallen from 76 percent and 75 percent respectively in 1965 to 43 percent in both for 1980. Industries new to the county include metals, electrical, and rubber. New capital expenditures have risen consistently and sharply through most of the period covered (Table III-41). The only exception to similarities between the two counties is the changes in general population. Troup County experienced declines in population prior to 1970 with recent growth of 12.4 percent, and Muscogee County experienced much of its growth from 1950 to 1960 with slower growth more recently (Table III-38). Otherwise, both counties appear primed for new economic development.

TABLE III-44

Muscogee County, Georgia
Manufacturing Employment and Payroll by Selected Industry
1965–1980

	Employment[a]				Payroll[b]			
	1965	1970	1975	1980	1965	1970	1975	1980
County	16,375	16,920	—	18,568	16,945	22,875	—	58,357
Furniture	—	104	—	—	—	139	—	—
Stone, Clay, & Glass	181	233	—	399	159	262	—	772
Metals	578[d]	660	—	1079[d]	652[d]	1062	—	3577[d]
Machinery	713	432[e]	—	1312	818	1000[e]	—	4116[e]
Electrical	—	—	—	500–999	—	—	—	—
Food	3078	3304	—	3995	3504	5289	—	13,858
Textiles	9653	9235	—	7342	9590	11,153	—	22,112
Apparel	[e]	581	—	184	[e]	617	—	439
Paper	—	[e]	—	69	—	[e]	—	204[e]
Chemicals	136	245	—	100–249	138	283	—	[e]
Rubber	—	[e]	—	250–499	—	[e]	—	[e]

Source: Bureau of the Census, U.S. Dept. of Commerce, *County Business Patterns,* 1965, 1970, 1975, 1980.
[a] Number of employees for week including March 12; no data available for 1975.
[b] First quarter only in $ thousands; no data available for 1975.
[c] SIC 33 only.
[d] SIC 34 only.
[e] Withheld to avoid disclosing information for individual companies.

Whitfield County (Labor area: Dalton, Georgia)

In contrast to the other three counties presented for Georgia, Whitfield County has experienced general prosperity over the past fifteen years. With general population consistently increasing over 19 percent per decade since 1950 (Table III-38), new capital expenditures increasing between 1963 and 1982 (Table III-41), and manufacturing employment exhibiting growth of 47.2 percent over the period 1965 to 1980 (Table III-46), Whitfield County's future is bright. Indeed, with the exception of apparel, all the industries presented in Table III-46 have shown positive growth. Even textile employment, which has suffered in most other counties in North Carolina, South Carolina, and Georgia, grew 68.7 percent over the period 1965 to 1980, accounting for 76 percent of the county's manufacturing employment and 78 percent of its manufacturing payroll in 1980. It is unlikely that textile management in Whitfield County is faced with concerns of competing against other industry in local labor markets.

Two of the four counties presented for Georgia exhibit industrial realignment towards high technology, high paying industry. The

Employee Relations in the Textile Industry

TABLE III-45

Troup County, Georgia
Manufacturing Employment and Payroll by Selected Industry
1965–1980

	Employment[a]				Payroll[b]			
	1965	1970	1975	1980	1965	1970	1975	1980
County	7538	8080	7536	10,067	7017	11,550	14,943	33,294
Furniture	—	—	—	—	—	—	—	—
Stone, Clay, & Glass	203	—	223	53	235	—	429	121
Metals	—	—	—	378[d]	—	—	—	1120[d]
Machinery	e	e	688	632	e	e	1816	2531[e]
Electrical	—	—	—	100–249	—	—	—	
Food	142	233	20–99	20–99	106	315	e	e
Textiles	5712	5484[e]	3356	4348	5257	7857[e]	6127[e]	14,467
Apparel	536	e	500–999	1118	378	e	e	2579
Paper	—	—	—	—	—	—	—	—
Chemicals	—	e	—	—	—	e	—	e
Rubber	—		391	250–499	—		683	

Source: Bureau of the Census, U.S. Dept. of Commerce, *County Business Patterns*, 1965, 1970, 1975, 1980.
[a] Number of employees for week including March 12.
[b] First quarter only in $ thousands.
[c] SIC 33 only.
[d] SIC 34 only.
[e] Withheld to avoid disclosing information for individual companies.

other two counties demonstrate the potential for continued dominance of the textile industry, with one county experiencing general prosperity and the other exhibiting declines in non-textile employment. In general, Georgia is realigning slowly in concert with the rest of the South.

SUMMARY

The textile industry, which once dominated employment in many southern communities, is being challenged as these communities' leading employer by high technology industries such as metals, machinery, electrical, chemicals, and rubber. Industrial realignment is evident in many of the counties presented in this chapter, although some counties demonstrate more a potential for industrial realignment than for mature diversification. The potential for and actualization of this realignment has prompted labor intensive industries, such as textiles, to respond with at least better wages or automation. Evidence of other responses will be presented in Chapter V.

TABLE III-46

Whitfield County, Georgia
Manufacturing Employment and Payroll by Selected Industry
1965–1980

	Employment[a]				Payroll[b]			
	1965	1970	1975	1980	1965	1970	1975	1980
County	14,036	16,609	15,267	20,667	14,799	23,357	29,575	63,867
Furniture	[e]	—	—	100–249	[e]	—	—	[e]
Stone, Clay, & Glass	189	138	121	219	162	191	235	579[d][e]
Metals	—	—	—	20–99[d]	—	—	—	
Machinery	255	751	341	421	314	1135	787	1419[e]
Electrical	—	—	—	100–249	—	—	—	
Food	486	451	250–499	569	485	559	[e]	1257
Textiles	9370	11,813	11,553	15,805	10,286	16,726	22,410	49,953
Apparel	2634	1221	427	336	2234	1205	499	799
Paper	—	—	71	189	—	—	151	706
Chemicals	100	200	145	313	164	429	505	1049
Rubber	405	632	631	474	597	1274	1524	1585

Source: Bureau of the Census, U.S. Dept. of Commerce, *County Business Patterns,* 1965, 1970, 1975, 1980.
[a] Number of employees for week including March 12.
[b] First quarter only in $ thousands.
[c] SIC 33 only.
[d] SIC 34 only.
[e] Withheld to avoid disclosing information for individual companies.

The survey instrument (see Questionnaire, Appendix I) attempted to discover how much of an impact the respondent thought that industrial development in the South, and particularly in the specific location, had influenced decisions that had been made in the personnel/employee relations function in the past decade. Table III-47 shows that approximately two-thirds of the respondents (65.2 percent) thought that industrial development had made a moderate to significant impact on the personnel area. The fact that 32.5 percent of the respondents (28 out of 86) thought there had been no impact or minimal impact arising out of industrial development in the area indicates that there is still a sizable number of plants operating in locations in the three states studied where industrial development awaits a new course of events in the future. The respondents were asked to indicate the extent that their specific company had changed personnel/industrial relations policies in response to industrial development and, again, approximately two-thirds (61.6 percent), indicated that the impact had only been moderate to significant. It is noteworthy, however, that 38.4 percent of the respondents (31) indicated that their company/plant had not been affected or was

TABLE III-47

Impact of Industrial Development on
Textile Industrial Relations

Overall Perceptions

28 Companies, 86 Plants

Response	Local Impact of New Industrial Development[a]		Company/Plant Reaction to New Industrial Development[b]	
	Number	Percent	Number	Percent
None	2	2.3	4	4.7
Minimal	26	30.2	27	31.4
Moderate	34	39.6	38	44.2
Significant	22	25.6	15	17.4
Unknown	2	2.3	2	2.3

Source: Industrial Research Unit Textiles Questionnaire.
[a] See Questionnaire in Appendix (Question No. 32).
[b] See Questionnaire in Appendix (Question No. 33).

minimally affected by new industrial development. These findings support the conclusion that a surprisingly large number of textile facilities are still located in places where they continue to be somewhat isolated from the mainstream of industrial development in the states studied. This could change rather quickly over the next decade, however, if consolidation and mergers continue in the textile industry. Plant closures and cutbacks in employment could lead to a welcoming and recruitment of new industrial activity into previously textile-dominant locations.

CHAPTER IV

Unionization

The United States textile industry is labor intensive and it has witnessed a slow evolvement over its 190-year history. Employers in the industry remain firmly committed to a union free environment, and one that places considerable importance on the unilateral right to determine wages, hours and working conditions. This chapter addresses the status of unionization in the textile industry by analyzing the results of recent elections that have been conducted by the National Labor Relations Board. A brief historical summary is presented in order to place contemporary events in the proper perspective.

EFFORTS TO ORGANIZE PRIOR TO 1970

Union activity in the textile industry dates back to the early 19th century when societies of New England textile workers organized and struck for higher wages and shorter hours following the depression of 1819.[1] The new labor societies coincided with the revival of other unions, all of which were seeking a share of prosperity in the developing country. Early unionization was characterized by cyclical swings in the economy. During depressed economic conditions, individuals attempted to protect their own interests in any way possible and, during the upswing of the business cycle, union activity resurfaced and labor demand ensured some collective bargaining power.

Between 1822 and 1870, the textile industry encountered many strikes by unions such as the Factory Girl's Association (1836), the New England Working Men's Association (1844), and the Benevolent and Protective Association of United Operative Mule Spinners of New England (1858). Most of these strikes failed to gain any concessions, since the associations lacked adequate financing, expertise in planning strikes, and employers increasingly used im-

---

[1] Foster Rhea Dulles, *Labor in America* (New York: Thomas Y. Crowell Company, 1960), p. 32.

migrant labor to replace discontented workers.[2] In response to these failures, the textile unions attempted to organize along craft lines in the 1870s. The mule spinners were the first to organize in 1858 followed by the weavers in 1873, the card room workers in 1873, the slasher tenders in 1875, and the drawing-in girls in 1875. This strategy also failed to promote union control and power as evidenced in the demise of the weavers and the card room operatives during the 1875 Fall River strike.

The 1870s marked the first attempts at southern unionization in the textile industry. The secret organization of the Knights of Labor, founded in Philadelphia by a group of garment cutters in 1869, sought membership in Alabama, Kentucky, Georgia, North Carolina, and Florida.[3] The Knights of Labor had some success in the South and membership grew to approximately 45,700 for non-textile employees. The union efforts to organize textile mills for the purpose of gaining higher wages and shorter hours were met consistently with employer lockouts, discharges, and blacklisting. The Knights of Labor disappeared from the southern textile industry by 1890 having achieved only the planting of ideas pertaining to organization among mill workers.[4]

Union activity in the textile industry was minimal and continued to be quite ineffective between 1890 and 1898. In 1898, after the highly publicized failure of several independent locals acting cooperatively to gain concessions from several employers in Augusta, Georgia, these local unions applied to and became affiliated with the American Federation of Labor (AFL) as the National Union of Textile Workers (NUTW). This union reached a membership of 5,000 in 1900; however, the Augusta strike of 1902 broke the union and organization disappeared from southern textiles once more.[5]

In 1912, organizing activity renewed the formation of textile locals in Lynchburg and Danville, Virginia and Knoxville, Tennessee. These locals approached the United Textile Workers Union (UTW)[6] convention in 1913 with requests for membership and a national union, once again, pursued textile unionization in the South. It appeared that significant gains might be made when the UTW

---

[2] *Ibid.,* p. 76.

[3] F. Ray Marshall, *Labor in the South* (Cambridge: Harvard University Press, 1967), p. 21–22.

[4] George Sinclair Mitchell, *Textile Unionism in the South* (Chapel Hill: University of North Carolina Press, 1931), p. 24–25.

[5] *Ibid.,* p. 27.

[6] The United Textile Workers (UTW) had formed in the northeast in 1902 from remnants of the NUTW and the American Federation of Textile Operatives (AFTO). The AFTO had been founded in 1899 by New England crafts disenchanted with the NUTW.

membership grew from 18,000 in 1914 to 104,900 in 1920.[7] The recession of 1920–21 began and the unions failed completely with strikes in Elizabethton, Tennessee and Gastonia[8] and Marion, North Carolina. These failures resulted from inadequate financing, strike breaking, and government intervention following extreme violence. By 1929, textile unionism in the South had again receded.

Between 1930 and World War II, several significant events occurred, which led to sustained organization at the time, but which would eventually establish the unions which would persist up until the 1970s.

The first of these events was the UTW response to the failure of employers to abide by the National Industrial Recovery Act of 1933 (NIRA) which was developed as a part of Franklin D. Roosevelt's New Deal. This response took the form of a general strike called in 1934 in pursuit of a thirty-hour, five-day work week, a weekly wage of $13, elimination of the stretchout, recognition of the union as a bargaining agent of the textile industry, and creation of an arbitration board to adjust labor disputes. The strike began in August 1934 and lasted less than a month. It was estimated that as many as 450,000 workers struck, including 60,000 in Georgia and 28,000 in Alabama.[9] The UTW considered this solidarity inadequate and formed "flying squads" of strikers to close mills whose workers did not walk out. These squads spread violence across South Carolina and Georgia, and this resulted in Governor Eugene Talmadge of Georgia declaring martial law and deporting strikebreakers. This opposition, including local disappointment in the squad tactic, ultimately contributed to the UTW seeking government intervention to ensure at least partial success of the strike. President Roosevelt appointed the Textile Labor Relations Board to investigate violations of the NIRA and the strike ended. Since the Board proved ineffective, the workers viewed the settlement as a union defeat and union membership declined.

Another significant event prior to World War II occurred in 1937 when the diminished UTW, discredited by the 1934 strike, contracted with the CIO to permit the newly formed Textile Workers Organizing Committee (TWOC) organizational jurisdiction over textile workers. Although the UTW was hoping to use the TWOC to increase its own membership, what resulted in 1939 was the affil-

---

[7] Lewis L. Lorwin, *The American Federation of Labor: History, Policies, and Prospects* (The Brooking's Institution, Washington, D.C., 1933), p. 519.

[8] In 1928, the Communists formed the National Textile Worker's Union (NTWU). This union led the Gastonia strike which was marked by violence. This discredited union leadership and virtually destroyed the union.

[9] Dulles, *Labor in America*, p. 272; Marshall, *Labor in the South*, p. 167–178.

iation of the TWOC with the CIO as the Textile Workers Union of America (TWUA/CIO). At this time, the TWOC had grown from 15,000 members in 1937 to 235,000 in 1939. With the affiliation the TWUA became the predominant union in the textile industry and would persist as such in the ensuing decades.

The final major event for this prewar period occurred in 1939, when the AFL restarted the UTW around several of its own locals and dissident groups from the TWUA. By 1941, the UTW claimed a membership of 42,608,[10] which would subsequently grow during the war.

During World War II, the TWUA/CIO gained over 120,000 new members, including an organization of the largest cotton mill in the country at Dan River in Danville, Virginia. The gains for the TWUA included contracts with Irwin Mills and Harriet Mills both of North Carolina. The UTW-AFL also made gains during the war climbing to a membership of 60,000 by 1946. Much of the growth in both unions can be attributed to stimulation of a war economy and the establishment of the National War Labor Board in 1942 to settle disputes and stabilize wages. Despite the Board's avowed neutrality in labor-management relations, its policies favored union membership, and it essentially "could translate representation elections into contracts." [11]

Subsequent to World War II, organization attempts continued but there were very few gains accomplished. The UTW/AFL and the TWUA/CIO both mounted extensive southern organizing campaigns in this period. The UTW campaign ended in 1947 when union leadership decided that a combination of inadequate financing and anti-union legislation raised the uncertainty of success beyond acceptable limits. The TWUA campaign lasted until 1953 when it collapsed because of inadequate financing and political infighting.[12]

It appears that a long-standing rift between Emil Rieve and George Baldanzi, both important early activists and leaders in the TWUA/CIO, had a negative impact on textile organizing. The 1952 TWUA convention highlighted major difficulties between Rieve and Baldanzi. A slate of officers, offered by Baldanzi in opposition to the Rieve forces, were all defeated, and Baldanzi lost his challenge to Rieve to become president of the union. This defeat led Baldanzi to leave the TWUA to become director of organizing for the UTWA/AFL. The UTWA did not make major gains subsequent to these events; however, an important victory was achieved at Dan River,

---

[10] Marshall, *Labor in the South*, p. 235.

[11] *Ibid.*, p. 227.

[12] See Marshall, *Labor in the South*, pp. 259–61.

"where there were some 11,000 eligible voters, 7,700 of whom voted for the UTW, 1,624 for 'no union,' and 278 for the TWUA." [13] Professor F. Ray Marshall indicates that the "AFL gained less than 2,000 dues-paying members at Danville because many workers would not join the union and the company refused to grant a check-off." [14] Feuding between the two unions further weakened efforts to organize textile plants, although it appears that lack of financial support, uncooperative local government officials, and employer opposition would have ultimately led to defeat even if unions had developed a coordinated program.

In 1955, the AFL and CIO merged, and the TWUA emerged as the predominant textile union in the federation. The backing of the combined AFL and CIO did little to alter the direction of textile unionization in the South. The TWUA was severely defeated in 1958–1961 strike, marred by violence, at Harriet Henderson Mills in Henderson, North Carolina at a cost of approximately $1.5 million, and in 1956, Milliken's Darlington Manufacturing Company closed down in South Carolina which appeared to be retaliation against the workers who had selected the TWUA as their representative on September 6, 1956. The latter case led to filings of unfair labor practices by the TWUA which were sustained by the NLRB, the appellate courts, and the Supreme Court. The Darlington case resulted in more than a single defeat for the union. The union was so intimidated by this event that activity was diminished until the 1970s.

MAJOR EVENTS SINCE 1970

The most widely publicized union campaigns in recent decades have centered on organizing efforts at J.P. Stevens and Cannon Mills. The long-standing Darlington case at Milliken was finally settled in 1980.

J.P. Stevens

In 1963, while the Darlington case was still under court review, the TWUA began a new organizing drive against J.P. Stevens. From 1963 to 1975, the union lost 11 of 12 elections held at different Stevens' plants. The union's only victory came in 1974, when seven plants in Roanoke Rapids, North Carolina voted to affiliate with

---

[13] *Ibid.,* p. 260.
[14] *Ibid.*

the union "by a slim margin of 237 votes out of 3,205 cast." [15] Despite an apparent victory, the union failed to obtain any immediate concessions or contracts.

In 1976, the TWUA and the Amalgamated Clothing Workers of America (ACWA) passed merger resolutions which resulted in the formation of the Amalgamated Clothing and Textile Workers Union (ACTWU). The new union's reported membership reached 495,000 (TWUA—170,000 and ACWA—325,000).[16] Delegates and speakers at the merger convention in Washington, D.C. quickly pledged to continue the TWUA's organization drive at J.P. Stevens. During the ensuing four years, the union employed two new tactics in an attempt to pressure Stevens into accepting a contract. The first of these tactics was a consumer boycott. The ACWA had brought experience in boycott activities to the merger having successfully applied this tactic against the Farah Manufacturing Company in 1974.[17] Boycott activity against Stevens failed miserably. Evidently, the union did not appreciate the consumer's inability to associate company and product.[18] Indeed, only 34 percent of Stevens' products were sold retail at that time, and the boycott had no discernible impact on Stevens' financial position.[19]

The second tactic employed by the union, commonly referred to as the corporate campaign, was instituted in 1976. This campaign consisted of two devices. The first was directed at Stevens' management and the second at companies with director ties to Stevens. The first device consisted of adding two proposals to the agenda of the 1976 shareholder's meeting. The union used a sympathetic shareholder to request these proposals. The first of these proposals demanded that management publish its ongoing cost in the dispute with the ACTWU. The second demanded reconciliation between hourly and management pensions. Neither proposal passed, although the first attracted 800,000 votes and the second 500,000

[15] Terry W. Mullins and Paul Luebke, "Symbolic Victory and Political Reality in the Southern Textile Industry: The Meaning of the J.P. Stevens Settlement for Southern Labor Relations," *Journal of Labor Research*, Vol. III, No. 1 (Winter 1982), p. 82.
[16] "A Labor Merger Aimed at the South," *Business Week*, No. 2420 (February 23, 1976), pp. 28–29.
[17] "Boycott Battle to Win the South," *Business Week*, No. 2461 (December 6, 1976), pp. 80–82.
[18] A short discussion of consumer orientation is available in Richard L. Rowan, *The Negro in the Textile Industry* (Philadelphia: Industrial Research Unit, Wharton School of Finance and Commerce, University of Pennsylvania 1970), pp. 19–20.
[19] Terry W. Mullins and Paul Luebke, "Symbolic Victory and Political Reality in the Textile Industry: The Meaning of the J.P. Stevens Settlement for Southern Labor Relations," *Journal of Labor Research*, Vol. III No. 1 (Winter 1982), p. 83.

votes.[20] This tactic achieved significant publicity for the union. Indeed, this tactic has found increasing popularity in the 1980s among special interest groups desiring publicity.

The second device employed by the union met with even more success. This device designed by Ray Rogers, a union organizer and consultant, effectively led to several directorate resignations. James Finley, Stevens' CEO at that time, resigned as a director of Manufacturers Hanover Trust and New York Life Insurance. The union had threatened Manufacturers Hanover with withdrawal of its one billion dollars in assets if it continued to allow Finley a director's role. David Mitchell, chairman of Avon Products, Inc., resigned from the boards of both Stevens and Manufacturers Hanover. R. Manning Brown, Jr., chairman of New York Life, resigned from the Stevens' board. The union also threatened to nominate two directors to the board of Metropolitan Life Insurance Company because R.R. Shinn, CEO of Metropolitan Life, had chaired a committee to renominate James Finley as a director of Sperry Corporation. Although it is unlikely that the union's nominees would have won, Metropolitan Life would have had to spend about $9 million to accommodate the nominations.[21]

This last threat proved unnecessary when, on October 20, 1980, J.P. Stevens agreed to a two and one-half year contract with ACTWU. Management concessions in the contract included checkoff, arbitration of workplace conditions, and $3 million in withheld pay and benefit increases which had already been granted to other Stevens' employees. Union concessions included termination of boycott, corporate campaign, and NLRB cases against Stevens; limitation of organizing attempts directed at Stevens for 18 months; and a commitment not to single out Stevens as the union's primary textile industry target. Although the union claimed some measure of success from this settlement, it appears that it was a victory for management. This victory is evident from the facts that union employees receive no better wage and benefits than nonunion employees and that Stevens has kept the union in abeyance with only 10 percent of its workforce unionized and check-off ranges in union facilities from 6 percent to 65 percent.[22]

---

[20] "Union Gains Popular Support in its Battle Against Stevens," *Textile World,* Vol. 126, No. 4 (April 1976), pp. 23–24.

[21] "The Ripples Spreading from the Stevens Pact," *Business Week,* No. 2661 (November 3, 1980), p. 110.

[22] For additional discussion on the settlement's limited impact see the Mullins and Luebke article cited in footnote 15. This article discusses the settlement's impact on Stevens, the textile industry, and the South.

Milliken

Another significant development in textile unionization occurred on December 15, 1980, when Milliken and Company agreed to compensate former employees of Darlington Manufacturing for its closing of the plant in 1956. This closing came in retaliation for employees of Darlington Manufacturing in South Carolina voting 256 to 248 for representation by the TWUA on September 6, 1956. The plant was closed in mid-October and equipment was auctioned in December 1956. Upon petition, the NLRB ruled that the plant was not closed for economic reasons but as a warning to Deering-Milliken employees not to seek union representation. Subsequent appeals by Milliken were not successful since the Fourth Circuit sustained the NLRB ruling as did the Supreme Court which refused to hear the case.[23] Therefore, in December 1980, Milliken agreed to pay $5 million to former employees or their surviving relatives.[24] However, as in the Stevens settlement, this victory proved only to be symbolic. With awards ranging from $50 to $36,000 after 24 years, the employees received virtually insignificant retribution, and to this date Milliken does not have a single unionized employee.

Cannon Mills

On November 20, 1974 the National Labor Board conducted an election at Cannon plants in Cabarrus and Rowan Counties in the Kannapolis, North Carolina area. This was the largest election ever conducted in the textile industry, requiring some 31 polling places, and the TWUA lost their bid for representation by a vote of 8,473 to 6,801.[25] The close vote offered some encouragement, as well as disappointment, to the union accustomed to major defeats in the industry. According to a union spokesman, the interest in representation among employees was based on "the rising number of black employees, many of whom are 'more militant' about organization than are whites"; ". . . the business slump and reductions in

---

[23] Philip Sparks, "Darlington Case: Justice Delayed is Justice Denied, *Labor Law Journal,* Vol. 26, No. 12, December 1975, p. 759.

[24] "Former Textile Workers Approve a $5 Million Pact," *New York Times* (December 15, 1980), p. A15.

[25] Bureau of National Affairs, "Cannon Mills Employees Turn Down Textile Workers' Organizing Bid," *Daily Labor Report,* No. 226, November 21, 1974, p. A-2.

the workweek from an average six days to les than five"; and "bad business" which had affected pensions.[26]

Management officials gave a mixed response to the election outcome. The chairman of the board at Cannon, Don Holt, said the election results were "an expression of confidence by Cannon people and of the desire to continue working together to maintain a productive and successful manufacturing company." [27] A management spokesman for *Textile World* indicated that managers in the industry "are worried that the attitude of textile workers no longer is hostile to unionism." [28] These propositions waited to be tested once again in the 1980s.

In mid-1984, the ACTWU began a campaign at Cannon which culminated in an election on October 10, 1985. The union lost the election by a vote of 5,692 to 3,534.[29] Some observers thought that the election would be close based on the 1974 election, and that perhaps the union would win since the company had been purchased recently by financier, David H. Murdock, and a large number of employees had been dismissed.[30] The union campaign was unsuccessful in discrediting Mr. Murdock and in creating a belief on the part of employees that the union could protect jobs and improve working conditions in Cannon's Rowan and Cabarrus County plants.

The union was disappointed in the loss since it had not claimed a major organizing victory since it added 3,415 workers in 1974 as a result of the J.P. Stevens campaign in Roanoke Rapids, North Carolina. A win at Cannon could have lifted the union's spirits and possibly put the ACTWU back "on a growth path." [31] Bruce Raynor, director of the union's southeast region, said: "They ran an incredibly vicious campaign. Even the Stevens family never came down personally and threatened to close the mill." [32] Raynor remains optimistic and, like his predecessors, "contends that organizing Cannon is only a matter of time." [33] The union will have to carry its

[26] Bureau of National Affairs, "Some 16,000 Cannon Mills Employees to Vote on Representation by Textile Workers Union," *Daily Labor Report*, No. 217, November 8, 1974, p. A-9.
[27] Bureau of National Affairs, *Daily Labor Report*, No. 226, November 21, 1974, p. A-2.
[28] "Cannon 'Yes,' Union, 'No': Here's What It Means," *Textile World*, Vol. 124, No. 12, December 1974, p. 23.
[29] *Textile News*, Vol. 41, No. 4, October 21, 1985, pg. 1.
[30] Pete Engardio, "Why David Murdock is So Afraid of a Union," *Business Week*, (October 14, 1985), p. 43.
[31] Winston Williams, "David Murdock Beats the Union," *New York Times* (October 20, 1985), p. 27.
[32] *Ibid.*
[33] Engardio, "Why David Murdock ... ", page 83.

TABLE IV-1

Textile Industry
NLRB Representation Election Results by Year
1971–1980

Year	Number of Elections	Total Eligible Voters	Avg. Unit Size	Union Victory Percent	Union Yield Percent[a]
1971	1	320	320	100	100
1972	58	11,863	205	36	45
1973	68	13,961	205	38	26
1974	107	39,896	372	37	26
1975	40	4,476	112	38	54
1976	84	14,297	170	43	20
1977	86	10,010	116	35	35
1978	79	14,152	179	38	30
1979	64	12,208	191	33	15
1980	5	136	27	20	2

Source: Wharton Industrial Research Unit data bank of NLRB elections.
[a] (Total Eligible Voters in Units Won/Total Eligible Voters) × 100.

campaign to Fieldcrest if it wishes to attain this objective since Cannon was purchased by Fieldcrest shortly after the election.

RECENT NLRB ELECTION RESULTS

Historically, unions have been the most visible during periods when employees are concerned about their job security. Table IV-1 shows that for election result data over the period from late 1971 to early 1980, union election activity reached a peak during the 1974 recession with 107 elections involving 39,896 workers. Furthermore, in 1974, the average unit size per election grew to a high of 372 employees for the time frame presented. Not only does the union increase its activity during a recession, it tries to magnify this activity by simultaneously pursuing larger units. Although activity may have increased, the union's success rate did not change appreciably, remaining at 37 percent for 1974, followed by 38 percent in both 1973 and 1975. Therefore, in absolute terms, union activity seems to suggest increasing victories, since 37 percent of 107 elections is greater than 38 percent of 68 elections or 38 percent of 40 elections.

The yield factor must also be considered before activity can be assumed a good predictor of success. As defined in Table IV-1, yield is a measure of the size of the units won. A low yield means that the union is winning the smaller units; a high yield means that the larger unit is being won. In 1974, when 107 elections were held, the

TABLE IV-2

Textile Industry
NLRB Representation Election Results by Case Type
1971–1980

Type[a]	Number of Elections	Total Eligible Voters	Avg. Unit Size	Union Victory Percent	Union Yield Percent[a]
RC	552	118,035	214	37	28
RD	27	1,940	72	41	50
RM	13	1,344	103	38	36

Source: Computer tapes, NLRB Data Systems Branch.
[a] RC = Employee/Union petitioned certification.
RD = Employee petitioned decertification election.
RM = Management petitioned certification election.
[b] (Total Eligible Voters in Units Won/Total Eligible Voters) × 100.

yield amounted to only 26 percent. This is contrasted with one year later, 1975, when 40 elections were held and the yield was 54 percent. It appears that the more elections are conducted, the less the union can focus on any particular election and the less opportunity it has to wage sophisticated and probably lengthy battles against larger employers. Union successes are likely to be greater in smaller units, which are the units most vulnerable to economic downturn. Statistically, activity may not be a good predictor of either victory percentage or yield percentage. Other factors such as financing, management's sophistication in personnel administration, the number of union organizers involved, the size of the community, local economic climate and employee loyalty may impact success to a larger extent. Since by their nature these potential predictors preclude quantification, this section will be restricted to discussing the NLRB data presented.

Table IV-2 presents the election result data by case type. As would be expected, the majority of elections held originated as petitions for certification by either employees or the union. Likewise, the fewest cases presented are management petitioned certification elections. With only a union victory percentage of 38 percent and yield of 36 percent, it appears that management may be using its petition as a defensive measure, accelerating election dates to avoid costly and lengthy campaigns and therefore preempting the union's opportunity to build support.

With respect to decertification elections, the union's victory percentage and yield were the highest among the three case types presented. This is surprising, since decertification elections are usually not called unless management believes there is an excellent chance for success. This type of election may be more a test of union strength in anticipation of more involved drives later. Of course, the assumption here is that employees petition for elections at the covert urging of management.

Table IV-3 presents the election result data by state for the textile industry, with the three states selected for study—Georgia, North Carolina, and South Carolina—highlighted at the top of the Table. "Total eligible voters" and "union victory" were roughly the same in Georgia and North Carolina. More elections were held in Georgia (50) than in either North Carolina (34) or South Carolina (11). Only 11 elections were held in South Carolina with 4,022 eligible voters; however, "union victory" was 45 percent with only a 15 percent union yield. Union yields in Georgia and North Carolina were 20 percent and 26 percent, respectively.

As might be expected, the Southeast accounted for most of the total eligible voters with Alabama, Florida, Georgia, North Carolina, and Tennessee representing all the states with 7,500 or more eligible voters each. This small group of states alone accounted for 57 percent of the total eligible voters. Furthermore, Arizona was the only one of the top seven states with respect to average unit size not located in Southeast. This indicates that since the Southeast represented a majority of the total eligible voters and it represented states with large unit sizes, it also represented states with a low relative number of elections per voter base. In fact, the five states mentioned earlier, which represented 57 percent of the total eligible voters, only accounted for 26 percent of the elections. Interestingly, seven Northeastern states, including Connecticut, Massachusetts, New Jersey, New York, Pennsylvania, Rhode Island, and Vermont, accounted for 31 percent of the elections but only 16 percent of the total eligible voters. Unions reveal a propensity for geographic dispersal whether or not it is cost motivated. Apparently, unions find it easier to campaign against small units in the Northeast than small units in the Southeast. Finally, Table IV-3 shows that nationwide, union victory percentage is 37 percent with a yield of 28 percent. Unions have more success organizing the smaller textile units rather than the larger units. Again, this may be a function of several variables, one of which may be more sophisticated personnel management in larger textile organizations.

Table IV-4 presents the election results data geographically by NLRB region. As anticipated, those regions which lead in total eligible voters are all located in the Southeast (Atlanta, Winston-Salem, and New Orleans); those regions with the highest victory percentages and the highest yield percentages were not located in

TABLE IV-3

Textile Industry
NLRB Representation Election Results by State
1971–1984

State	Number of Elections	Total Eligible Voters	Avg. Unit Size	Union Victory Percent	Union Yield Percent[a]
Three States Studied					
Georgia	50	11,220	224	34	20
North Carolina	34	11,224	330	35	26
South Carolina	11	4,022	366	45	15
Other States					
Unknown	16	1,988	124	25	11
Alabama	51	13,933	273	35	32
Arizona	10	2,037	204	80	55
Arkansas	13	1,962	151	15	7
California	97	7,358	76	37	35
Colorado	7	446	64	71	87
Connecticut	9	621	69	44	36
D.C.					
Delaware	1	61	61	0	0
Florida	10	1,081	108	40	30
Idaho	1	57	57	0	0
Illinois	28	3,335	120	36	21
Indiana	11	689	63	36	27
Iowa	3	88	29	33	56
Kansas	2	110	55	50	26
Kentucky	22	5,308	241	32	28
Louisiana	6	1,472	245	33	33
Maine	5	587	117	40	23
Maryland	14	1,373	98	21	08
Massachusetts	18	3,745	208	11	07
Michigan	24	1,364	57	42	35
Minnesota	10	549	55	40	29
Mississippi	24	6,365	265	33	17
Missouri	29	2,497	86	48	63
Montana	2	150	75	0	0
Nebraska	2	171	86	100	100
New Hampshire	1	114	114	100	100
New Jersey	36	2,213	61	42	36
New York	73	2,858	39	53	54
North Dakota	2	170	85	50	4
Ohio	25	2,518	101	20	34
Oklahoma	4	393	98	50	55
Oregon	6	223	37	50	30
Pennsylvania	55	4,454	81	33	24
Puerto Rico	11	1,570	143	27	32
Rhode Island	6	239	40	67	82
South Dakota					
Tennessee	41	10,816	264	24	26
Texas	11	1,874	170	9	1
Utah	3	133	44	67	57
Vermont	3	386	129	67	88
Virginia	29	8,009	276	48	27
Washington	9	294	33	0	0
West Virginia	5	976	195	40	51
Wisconsin	14	1,222	87	21	17
Total	845	122,313	145	37	28

Source: Wharton Industrial Research Unit data bank of NLRB elections.
[a] (Total Eligible Voters in Units Won/Total Eligible Voters) × 100.

TABLE IV-4

Textile Industry
NLRB Representation Election Results by NLRB Region
1971–1984

Region	Number of Elections	Total Eligible Voters	Avg. Unit Size	Union Victory Percent	Union Yield Percent
Boston, MA	42	5476	130	.3571	.1991
New York, NY	31	621	200	.6452	.6683
Buffalo, NY	17	1034	608	.5294	.6335
Philadelphia, PA	49	4031	82	.2653	.1789
Baltimore, MD	45	11289	250	.4000	.3464
Pittsburgh, PA	14	1072	76	.5000	.4049
Detroit, MI	22	1249	57	.4091	.2746
Cleveland, OH	8	334	42	.2500	.4641
Cincinnati, OH	43	8366	194	.2791	.3225
Atlanta, GA	99	25019	253	.3434	.2474
Winston-Salem, NC	52	16510	317	.3462	.2149
Tampa, FL	7	547	78	.5714	.6015
Chicago, IL	17	1485	87	.3529	.2909
St. Louis, MO	22	2237	102	.5000	.6366
New Orleans, LA	32	9200	287	.2188	.1962
Fort Worth, TX	12	1695	141	.3333	.1357
Kansas City, MO	15	852	57	.5333	.6279
Minneapolis, MN	14	592	42	.4286	.4054
Seattle, WA	9	299	33	.0000	.0000
San Francisco, CA	8	639	80	.5000	.1831
Los Angeles, CA	64	4941	77	.3438	.3228
Newark, NJ	31	1870	60	.4516	.4107
Houston, TX	4	575	144	.0000	.0000
Santurce, P.R.	12	1675	139	.2500	.3045
Indianapolis, IN	11	689	63	.3636	.2743
Memphis, TN	55	10588	192	.2727	.1732
Denver, CO	11	883	80	.7273	.8675
Albuquerque, NM	9	1795	199	.7778	.4953
Brooklyn, NY	30	1486	49	.4000	.3371
Milwaukee, WI	15	1359	91	.2000	.2252
Los Angeles, CA	18	1321	73	.3889	.5821
Oakland, CA	8	517	65	.3750	.1296
Peoria, IL	6	1506	251	.1667	.0046
Portland, OR	6	233	39	.3333	.2704
Honolulu, HI	2	84	42	.5000	.4524
Peoria, IL	3	169	56	.3333	.5444
Hartford, CT	2	75	37	.5000	.2267
Totals	845	122,313	145	.3680	.2754

Source: Wharton Industrial Research Unit data bank of NLRB elections.

the Southeast (New York, Seattle, San Francisco, Phoenix, and
Oakland); and those regions with the largest unit sizes, with the
exception of one election in Peoria, were exclusively Southeastern
(Atlanta, Winston-Salem, New Orleans, and Houston). In fact, only

TABLE IV-5

Textile Industry
NLRB Representation Election Results, Right to Work Analysis
1971–1984

Class	Number of Elections	Total Eligible Voters	Avg. Unit Size	Union Victory Percent	Union Yield Percent[a]
RTW	302	74,687	247	36	25
Non-RTW	543	47,626	87	37	31

Source: Wharton Industrial Research Unit data bank of NLRB elections.
[a] (Total Eligible Voters in Units Won/Total Eligible Voters) × 100.

one of the twenty-two regions presented with an average unit size less than 100 was located in the Southeast (Tampa-78). Therefore, presentation of the election results by NLRB region does not appear to be inconsistent with a presentation by state, even though some NLRB regions cross state lines.

Table IV-5 summarizes the election result data by right-to-work (RTW) and non right-to-work (Non-RTW) states. As the data indicate, the union victory percentage and union yield percentage are higher for Non-RTW, albeit only by a few points. Although it might be suggested that since there were more total eligible voters and larger average unit sizes in the RTW class and hence more absolute union yield, it must be remembered that by definition, even if the union wins the unit in RTW areas, an employee is not required to abide by the checkoff system for union dues. Since most checkoffs in RTW are less than 60 percent of union members, if not somewhat smaller, the union's success in RTW areas is poor.

Table IV-6 presents the election result data for unions which participated in ten or more elections during the period late 1971 to early 1984. As is apparent, the textile industry is subject to organizing efforts by unions other than those whose members are primarily textile employees. Indeed, the Teamsters union led the field with 130 elections involving 20,321 eligible voters.

Among the two remaining "textile" unions, the UTW conducts fewer elections than the ACTWU and the UTW appears to be slightly more successful in acquiring/retaining membership. In fact, it is probably this latter aspect of retaining membership for which the UTW is better known. This union has been described as docile and quite accommodating at the bargaining table. This is in contrast to ACTWU, which held seventy-one elections in its period of exist-

TABLE IV-6

Textile Industry
NLRB Representation Election Results, By Unions With Ten
Elections or More
1971–1984

Union	Number of Elections	Total Eligible Voters	Avg. Unit Size	Union Victory Percent	Union Yield Percent[a]
Autoworkers	16	1,512	95	25	18
Carpenters	8	431	54	38	28
Amalgamated Clothing and Textile Workers	261	51,124	196	36	26
Ladies Garment Workers	153	19,333	126	35	28
Meat Cutters	6	714	119	40	58
Paperworkers	10	1,477	148	40	44
Rubber Workers	9	1,575	175	29	9
Steelworkers	15	3,064	204	40	21
Teamsters	143	15,659	110	34	21
United Textile Workers	12	2,131	178	25	7

Source: Wharton Industrial Research Unit data bank of NLRB elections.
[a] (Total Eligible Voters in Units Won/Total Eligible Voters) × 100.

ence from 1976 to early 1980, and has been more aggressive at the
table and in getting to the table.

Summary

This chapter has explored unionization in the textile industry
through an historical presentation and an analysis of recent representation election results. Historically, the unions have failed to
penetrate the United States textile industry, particularly in the
South. This failure has resulted from repeated advances and re-
treats. Of course, not all of the failure can be attributed to union
ineptitude. Much of the failure is the result of management sophistication and expertise in aggressively responding to union
advances. These responses have included comprehensive communication programs, compensation and benefit upgrades, and consistency in policy formulation and application. As Chapter V will point
out, however, the myriad of small textile firms are still quite vulnerable to organization since they lack the sophistication of the
larger firms in developing and administering personnel policies.

CHAPTER V

Employment Policies and Practices in the Textile Industry

As noted in Chapter I, a questionnaire pertaining to employment policies and practices in the textile industry was completed by eighty-six responding units representing twenty-eight companies located in twenty-six counties within North Carolina, South Carolina, and Georgia. These responses to the questionnaire reflect employment activity in those areas of the country where a majority of the textile industry is concentrated. The eighty-six responding units represented returns by seventy-seven plants, and six companies reporting nine multi-plant facilities wherein employment figures were stated on an aggregate basis. For example, one of the companies reported a combined plant figure of 18,250 employees actually representing nineteen plants in a major complex.

Figure V-1 shows that over 50 percent (forty-three) of the responding seventy-seven plants had fewer than 500 hourly employees with 86 percent (sixty-six) employing fewer than 1,000. These data appear to support the dominance of relatively small plants in the industry. Large firms appear to be organized in small operating facilities. Small plant organization may be the result of task design, but it appears that a strong argument can be made for the fact that smaller units are more easily managed, and this may ensure that the firm is less vulnerable to large-scale union organizing efforts. Union organizing costs, to a large extent, do not vary with unit size. The textile firms are forcing the unions to gamble larger relative costs in proportion to the potential gains.[1]

Figure V-2 presents the number of salaried employees for the same facilities as presented in Figure V-1. Approximately 50 percent (forty-one) of the seventy-seven plants have fewer than fifty salaried employees with over 70 percent (fifty-four) employing fewer than 100 salaried employees. It appears that there is a low ratio of salaried to hourly employees in the textile industry. When we consider

---

[1] James B. Quinn, "Strategic Change: Logical Incrementalism," *Sloan Management Review,* Vol. 20, No. 1, Fall 1978.

FIGURE V-1

Textile Industrial Relations
Hourly Employment
22 Companies, 77 Plants

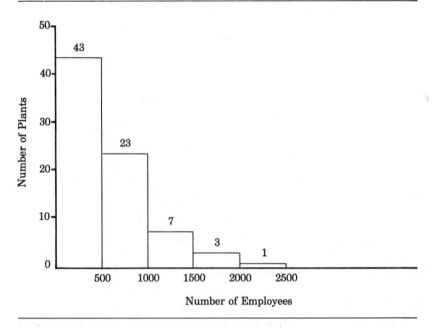

Source: Industrial Research Unit Textiles Questionnaire

that there are several levels of management and support staff, for example, accounting, research and development, and legal services, within the salaried ranks, it appears that there is a relatively small number of individuals in supervisory roles in the plants. This matter will be given further consideration later in this study.

Figure V-3 presents the number of part-time employees for the same facilities presented in Figures V-1 and V-2. As shown, 70 percent (forty-one) of the plants have fewer than twenty part-time employees with 93 percent (seventy-three) employing fewer than forty part-time employees. Also, 86 percent of the plants reported that the number of part-time workers is not increasing. It appears that the textile industry will not follow the lead of the low margin industries and employ a large number of part-timers to keep benefit costs low. Indeed, as discussed in Chapter II, the textile industry is focusing on automation and productivity improvements to keep labor requirements and associated labor costs contained. Part-time

FIGURE V-2

Textile Industrial Relations
Salaried Employment
22 companies, 77 plants

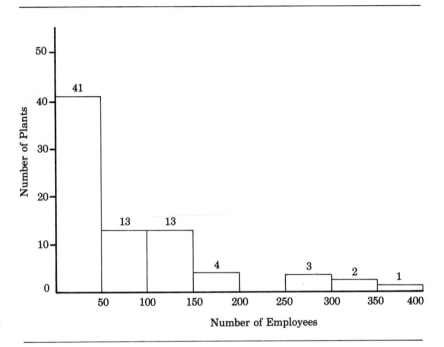

Source: Industrial Research Unit Textiles Questionnaire

employment seems to be confined to an occasional use of high school students by some employers and to a few companies that operate mini-shifts.

MANAGING THE PERSONNEL FUNCTION

The management of human resources is an important activity in a labor intensive industry such as textiles. As noted earlier in this study, a large majority of the employees in the industry consists of production workers classified as semi-skilled machine operators and unskilled laborers. These employees work in a variety of plant situations throughout the industry. The results of this study highlight the problems and practices associated with plant personnel management in the textile industry. In order to assess the problems and issues associated with plant personnel management, it is necessary

FIGURE V-3

Textile Industrial Relations
Part-time Employment
22 companies, 77 plants

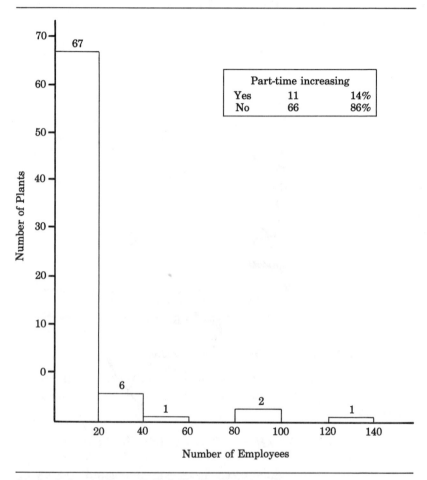

Part-time increasing		
Yes	11	14%
No	66	86%

Source: Industrial Research Unit Textiles Questionnaire

to review briefly the organization of the personnel function at the corporate level where policy is generally formulated.

Our survey included twenty-eight companies ranging in size from several hundred to thousands of employees and from those with a few to those with a large number of plants. All companies reported a chief personnel officer at corporate level with a title of manager, director, or vice president of personnel, industrial relations or human resources management. In most instances, these individuals report directly to the president/chief executive officer of the company in a staff relationship. Most have a functional relationship to the plant personnel manager who generally reports to the plant manager. A few of the companies reported a divisional organization wherein a division personnel manager reports to a division president; in turn, the division president reports to the chief executive of the company.

The chief personnel officer in the company identifies his major responsibilities as those of developing and administering policies and programs including areas such as employee relations, benefits and salaries, employment and personnel development, employee safety and health (OSHA), equal employment opportunity (EEO), affirmative action (AAP), community relations, and security. All respondents to our survey indicated that personnel policy is highly centralized at the corporate level. In the case of multi-plant companies, personnel policy is coordinated at the company headquarters level. There appears to have been an upgrading in recent years of the personnel function in companies studied. Outside pressures arising from government regulations, union organizing activities, and a changing economic and labor market environment have created a need for professional personnel management in the textile industry.

A unique feature in the organization of personnel management in the textile industry is the major emphasis on keeping the plants nonunion. This pervasive objective has led to the extensive utilization of outside legal counsel in the industry. In some instances, it appears that legal advice has been substituted for professional, in-house industrial relations/personnel management. In addition to union avoidance, outside legal expertise is utilized in areas such as affirmative action, equal employment opportunity, occupational safety and health, and the development and implementation of training programs. Some respondents in our study indicated that more inside legal counsel and increased reliance on professional personnel/industrial relations expertise within the company would be less expensive and more effective in dealing with the human resources function.

The survey of textile plants indicates that the chief personnel officer at the plant level is a personnel manager who reports directly to the plant manager. The personnel manager assists the plant manager in the interpretation and implementation of personnel policy formulated at the corporate level.

Less than one-half of the responding plants indicated that the personnel manager participated in the formulation of corporate personnel policy in any manner; however, all plants responded that the personnel manager was responsible for implementing policy at the plant level. It appears that the effectiveness of plant personnel managers could be enhanced if they were provided a more extensive opportunity to participate in policy formulation at the corporate level. In general, feedback systems seem to be underdeveloped and in need of fine tuning in order for top management to capture the expertise and knowledge present at the plant site.

There is a clear indication that textile personnel managers see their major role as that of enhancing the economic objectives of the company. Personnel is expected to work effectively with production toward achieving profit maximization. A close, interacting relationship between personnel managers and plant managers is considered vital to overall operations in the textile industry.

One plant official summarized the responsibilities of the plant personnel managers in the following manner: "To develop and maintain a good labor-management relationship within the organization by following company policies in a consistent and fair manner." Respondents specified some or all of the following responsibilities as part of the personnel manager's job: salary and benefits administration; the implementation of the employment function including recruiting, selection, orientation, hiring, training and development, and discipline; safety and health; affirmative action and equal employment opportunity; community and government relations; labor relations; and plant security.

IMPLEMENTING MANPOWER POLICY

Previous sections of this study examined the breakdown of hourly, salaried, and part-time employees in the plants investigated. This section will discuss personnel practices in the textile industry including recruiting, training, promotion policy, turnover, and unionization. Absenteeism, a fifth manpower issue, will be discussed in a following section on scheduling.

Recruitment

Personal references and walk-ins are heavily employed as recruiting methods by all of the plants sampled. Of all the plants, personal referrals are used 48.4 percent of the time, walk-ins 40.6 percent, college visits 2.3 percent, advertising 5 percent, and employment agencies 3.7 percent of the time. At least one plant reported that

it used personal referrals 95 percent of the time and another reported using walk-ins 85 percent of the time. Given the nature of
the textile industry, this should not come as a real surprise. First,
the more expensive vehicles are used least. Second, most firms use
college visits, advertising, and employment agencies in salaried recruiting rather than hourly recruiting. Since salaried employees
are considerably fewer in number than hourly employees, these
latter vehicles are employed less. A few firms, however, particularly
those needing to look outside the local community, do use visits to
technical schools, out-of-town advertising, and employment agencies
to a larger degree. Third, many authors have previously cited cases
where whole families have been employed in the mills. In the small,
closely knit southern communities, an employer need do no more
than announce an opening to his present employees, and a suitable
applicant is likely to be found. Finally, through task design, many
textile firms have eliminated the need for extensive education and
skills for entry level positions. As a result, most personal referrals
and walk-ins meet the minimal qualifications required. There is no
reason to pursue more costly recruiting methods.

Hiring and Training Policy and Practice

Table V-1 highlights the characteristics of hiring and training
policy and practices found in the industry. As this table shows, 79
percent of the responding plants indicated that they have minimum
qualifications for employment including an ability to read and write,
physical qualification, and/or a high school diploma/equivalency.
Most plants indicated that minimum qualification did vary by position. Included in the 21 percent that had no minimum qualifications[2] were mostly smaller plants/companies which cannot afford
to be as selective since their cost structures do not support the
compensation and benefit packages which the larger firms provide.

Once employees are hired, most of the responding plants indicated
that they provide training either on the job or through a structured
training department program. While in these programs, 51 percent
of new employees were paid less than full wage for the job class to
which the training would lead, and 93 percent were subject to dis-
missal if they failed to perform adequately during the probationary
period. Both the probation, and its associated differential, are sound
cost-effective measures for ensuring compatability between the new

---

[2] Several of the questionnaires indicated as a minimal qualification, "the ability
to breathe." These several responses were restricted to smaller independent firms
and were interpreted as no minimal qualification.

TABLE V-1

Textile Industrial Relations
Hiring/Training
28 Companies, 86 Plants[a]

Minimum Qualifications				*Probation Period*		
	Number	Percent			Number	Percent
Yes	67	79		Yes	80	93
No	18	21		No	6	7
Unknown	1					

Training Differential				*Training Program*		
	Number	Percent			Number	Percent
Yes	42	51		OJT	53	65
No	41	49		Training Department	29	35
Unknown	3			Unknown	4	

[a] Data include responses of 28 companies covering policy and practices in 86 plants.
Source: Industrial Research Unit Textiles Questionnaire.

employee and both the job and company. Furthermore, almost all probationary periods have significantly reduced benefit coverage to guard against abusers. In fact, qualification periods may extend beyond the initial probationary period to avoid significant investments in individuals who may turnover quickly.

Turnover

With respect to turnover, Figure V-4 and Table V-2 show that the approximate 30 percent average turnover experienced in the plants studied has generally stabilized with 90.5 percent of the plants indicating that turnover was under control. This manageability is further emphasized by the fact that over 70 percent of plants reported that turnover impact on their operations was minimal to nonexistent. If the response of moderate impact is included, the 72.3 percent rate grows to 97.6 percent.

How has the industry accommodated high average turnover? One would suspect through task design and training programs and, indeed, both the data and personal interviews bear this out. What may be surprising to the outsider, however, is not the adaptive accommodation of the industry to turnover, but the acceptance of

FIGURE V-4

Textile Industrial Relations Turnover
28 Companies, 86 Plants
(Percent)

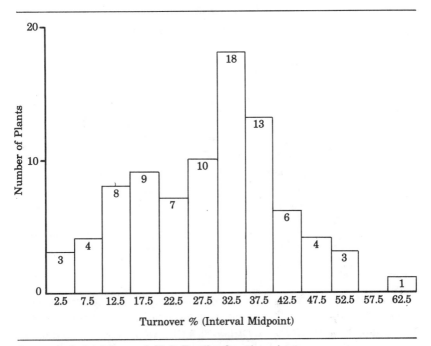

Source: Industrial Research Unit Textiles Questionnaire

turnover as a management strategy in some instances. Jobs have been designed to prevent disruption should an employee resign. But, designing in simplicity is equivalent to designing out challenge. Since companies can usually restructure tasks to permit greater challenge and provide a measure of self-fulfillment, there must be another motive for managing turnover rather than reducing it where this practice is found. This motive is cost. In order to remain competitive with foreign imports, some companies appear to have used turnover and probationary periods, probationary differentials, and benefits qualification to keep labor costs at a minimum. The expectation is that employees will not remain with the firm long enough to accrue costly benefits. Not all firms practice this (the minimum turnover was an insignificant 2 percent), and those that do (the maximum turnover reported was 60 percent) are responding to competition to promote their own survival.

TABLE V-2

Textile Industrial Relations
Turnover Perceptions
28 Companies, 86 Plants

Turnover Increasing

	Number	Percent
Yes	8	9.5
No	77	90.5
Unknown	1	

Turnover Impact

	Number	Percent
None	35	42.5
Minimal	25	30.1
Moderate	21	25.3
Significant	2	2.4
Unknown	3	

Source: Industrial Research Unit Textiles Questionnaire

Promotion Policy

In addition to activities in regard to turnover, another expected response to an extremely competitive environment is the movement by employeers toward a merit-based promotion policy. As Table V-3 shows, 67.3 percent of the responding plants promoted using a merit-based program with 18.4 percent using only seniority. Surprisingly, thirty-seven of the eighty-six responses did not address the promotion policy inquiry. In these cases, it can be inferred that the plants promote on a less systemized basis. Finally, among the

TABLE V-3

Textile Industrial Relations
Factors Utilized in Promotion Policy
28 Companies, 86 Plants

Promotion Factor	Number of Responding Plants	Percent of Responding Plants
Seniority	9	18.4
Merit	13	26.5
Merit, then Seniority	20	40.8
Other	7	14.3

Source: Industrial Research Unit Textiles Questionnaire

thirty-three plants using a merit-based program, it was interesting to find that thirteen plants used merit only. The management in these plants were admitting that no two employee's performance is so alike that seniority need be used as a differentiator.

Unionization

The last manpower issue to be considered in this section pertains to unionization. As mentioned in Chapter IV, the textile industry is much more union free than the conventional wisdom allows. Only five of the twenty-eight companies studied reported the presence of union contracts in their plants. A total of ten plants were found to be covered under union contracts. Eight of the ten unionized plants were organized prior to 1950, and they are all part of large, well-established textile firms. Interestingly, most of the unionized plants reported that less than 50 percent of the union members were paying dues to the union. Decertification may be expected in these situations; however, employers have decided to avoid this course of action in dealing with the union. Apparently, there is a strong belief that a decertification election may cause the employees to vote for the union even though they have not been paying dues into it for some time and creating an issue, through a decertification election, may lead to the employees joining another union which may be more difficult to manage.

Responses to our survey indicated that there had been some union activity in seven companies, representing twelve plant locations, in the period since 1979. Most of these union activities included hand-billing of employees, union sponsored employee meetings, and efforts on the part of the union to strengthen its current position in an existing unionized setting. Union activity was mainly generated by the Amalgamated Clothing and Textile Workers Union (ACTWU) but some activity was found by the United Automobile Workers Union (UAW) and the United Textile Workers Union (UTW). Our study indicates that organizing activity had taken place in large plants of large companies in the industry. When the union has targeted large plants of large companies, they have been met with formidable opposition by management which has used labor consultants and outside law firms to ensure a union-free environment. Surprisingly, the union has not developed major campaigns in small plants of small companies where it would appear it could have had more success in organizing. Some of the smaller plants have not been able to develop personnel systems on a sophisticated basis and they may not have the resources to oppose union organizing efforts. Large firms have sometimes been able to share their expertise in

TABLE V-4

Textile Industrial Relations
Shift Scheduling
28 Companies, 86 Plants

Continuous Shift			Shift Differential			Shift Types		
Yes	38	44%	Yes	66	78%	Fixed	69	80%
No	48	56%	No	19	22%	Rotating	13	15%
			Unknown	1		Both	4	5%

Most Frequent Shift Scheduled

Shifts	Days	Plants	Percent
1	4	0	0
1	5	3	3.5
2	5	4	4.7
2	6	0	0
2	7	0	0
3	5	47	54.7
3	6	13	15.1
3	7	5	5.8
	Other	14	16.2
		86	100.0

Source: Industrial Research Unit Textiles Questionnaire

the area of union avoidance with smaller neighbors with the hope that the unions will not be able to gain a sigificant geographical foothold.

SCHEDULING OF WORK

Table V-4 presents several characteristics of shift scheduling in the plants studied. The two most frequently implemented schedules were three shifts five days a week and three shifts six days a week. Together these two accounted for 69.8 percent of the plants. Taking into account those plants with three shifts seven days a week covered 65 of the 86 plants (75.6 percent). Therefore, most plants scheduled the day into three eight-hour shifts.

Table V-4 also indicates that thirty-eight plants (44 percent) operated on a twenty-four hour a day/seven days a week continuous shift basis. Excluding the five plants which most frequently scheduled three shifts seven days a week, the other thirty-three continuous shifts plants were found among the five and six day three shift operations and the "Other" category. These plants covered the balance of the week either by using twelve hour weekend shifts, by dividing short time among the other shifts, or by using part-time employees to supplement the work force.

Finally Table V-4 shows that most plants (80 percent) assigned fixed shifts and 78 percent paid a shift differential. Some companies indicated that it was not always necessary to pay a shift differential to maintain a labor force. The general state of the labor market would be a strong determining factor. Although rotating shifts might seem the fairest approach to scheduling, fixed shifts were generally favored by employees. First, some employees preferred to work second and third shifts. This preference usually originated from a need to be available during first shift hours to attend school or to take care of the family, although sometimes the preference was motivated by the shift differential. Second, a fixed shift program provided a non-monetary incentive to employees desiring either to remain on first shift or to move to first shift. At the same time, it also motivated individuals not to accept promotions requiring a shift change. In this latter case, however, as long as the employees understand the ramifications of their choice, the employer should feel justified in seeking other candidates.

Figure V-5 addresses the average weekly hours scheduled for the plants. As shown, the mode of the distribution was found in the interval where the midpoint was 40 hours per week. The mean was 41.9 hours per week with a maximum of 50 hours and a minimum of 32.0 hours. Slightly over 73 percent of the plants schedule overtime as a normal occurrence. Although not reported in the Figure, almost all plants paid more for overtime—usually time and a half or in some cases (i.e., holiday) double time. These differentials are less expensive to the employer than investing in new employees who may have to be laid off and recalled frequently in response to demand fluctuations.

Figure V-6 completes the scheduling discussion by presenting weekly lost hours *per employee* (unscheduled, unauthorized absenteeism or tardiness). Over 89 percent of the seventy-six plants which responded to this question had less than two lost hours per week. Quite amazingly, one plant experienced eight hours per week and another six hours per week. The plant which reported eight lost hours per week had an hourly workforce of fifty with a turnover of 10 percent. The plant which reported six lost hours per week had an hourly workforce of 2,700 and a turnover exceeding 27 percent. One plant was located in North Carolina and the other in South Carolina, and they were owned by different parent companies. It would be interesting to further explore management's response to such a turbulent labor situation.

FIGURE V-5

Textile Industrial Relations
Weekly Hours and Overtime
28 Companies, 86 Plants

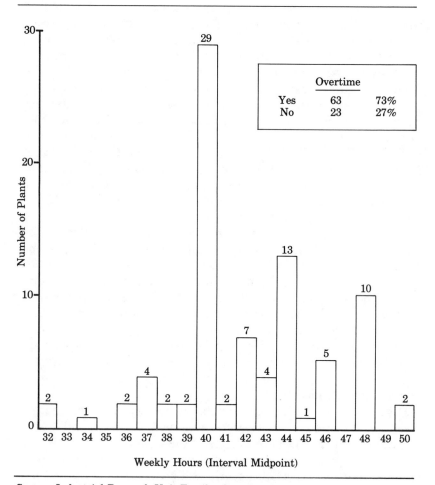

Source: Industrial Research Unit Textiles Questionnaire

WAGES AND BENEFITS

Table V-5 shows that 84.3 percent of the responding plants set wages in accordance with industry practice. Indeed, this policy is executed in a similar manner across a variety of industries, particularly regionally focused industries like automobiles, steel, or tex-

FIGURE V-6

Textile Industrial Relations
Weekly Lost Hours
28 Companies, 76 Plants

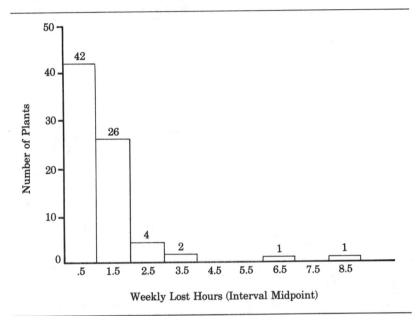

Weekly Lost Hours (Interval Midpoint)

Source: Industrial Research Unit Textiles Questionnaire

tiles. The importance of regional focus is that homogeniety in local environments can be assumed and significant cost of living differentials need not be provided. As Chapter II points out, however, textile wages are significantly lower than those for automobiles and

TABLE V-5

Textile Industrial Relations
Factors in Wage Setting Policy
28 Companies, 86 Plants

Factor	Number of Respondents	Percent of Known Practices
Industry Practice	59	84.3
Industry Leader	1	1.4
Local Developments	4	5.7
Union Contract	5	7.2
Other	1	1.4

Source: Industrial Research Unit Textiles Questionnaire

TABLE V-6

*Textile Industrial Relations
Benefits
28 Companies, 86 Plants*

Cost of Living Adjustments			Contributory Insurance		
	Number of Respondents	Percent		Number of Respondents	Percent
Yes	1	1.2	Medical	3	3.6
No	85	98.8	Life	7	8.4
			Both	16	19.3
			Company Paid	57	68.7

Retirement Programs			Why Retirement Program Changes		
	Number of Respondents	Percent		Number of Respondents	Percent
Company Paid	56	67.5	Competitive Pressure	27	65.9
Company Paid Accounting for Social Security	4	4.8	Inflation	6	14.6
			Cost	6	14.6
Employee Contribution plus Profit Sharing	12	14.5	Legislation	2	4.9
Company Paid plus Profit Sharing	11	13.2			

Source: Industrial Research Unit Textiles Questionnaire

steel. Where steel and automobile companies need not concern
themselves with other industries competing in their regional labor
market (since they are usually leaders), textiles, on the other hand,
is greatly concerned with local wage developments. With the rise
of higher wage industries in the Southeast (Chapter III), the textile
industry will grow increasingly vulnerable to these new competitors
in its once captive labor market. High turnover is evidence of this
vulnerability. Furthermore, since many of the employees attracted
away are the skilled operators and first line supervisors, the re-
placement costs borne by the textile industry are high both in
training expense and lost productivity. The industry should pay
close attention to local wage developments, although it cannot ig-
nore its position with respect to industry practice and the impact
of foreign competition.

Tables V-6 and V-7 summarize current benefit policies and practices in the textile industry. Cost of living adjustments (COLAs) are
virtually unheard of in the textile industry, with only one of the
86 responding plants indicating that it uses such an index. With

TABLE V-7

Textile Industrial Relations
Vacation, Holiday, and Personal Leave
28 Companies, 86 Plants

Response	Vacation		Holiday		Personal Leave	
	Number of Respondents	Percent	Number of Respondents	Percent	Number of Respondents	Percent
No			2	2.4	3	3.6
Yes Without Pay	1	1.2	1	1.2	4	4.8
Yes With Pay	83	98.8	78	92.8	76	91.6
Yes With and Without Pay			3	3.6		

Source: Industrial Research Unit Textiles Questionnaire

respect to insurance coverage, the industry is far more progressive than one might have originally expected. Only 20 percent of the plants required employee contributions to both life and medical insurance coverage. Over 68 percent of the plants provided company paid coverage, although in such cases a minimum deductible is usually applied. The remaining 12 percent of the plants required employee contributions to either life or medical insurance coverage. In almost all cases, however, there is a qualification period preceding coverage. Considering the high turnover in the industry and the pre-employment physicals, there is not much transient coverage issued or applied. This minimizes the company's investment even in company paid plans.

A third benefit studied was retirement and the reasons why retirement programs have changed progressively in recent years. As Table V-6 indicates, over 80 percent of the plants provided company paid retirement. Company paid plans were separated into company paid only (fifty-six plants), company paid less a social security adjustment (four plants), and company paid plus profit sharing provisions. Twelve plants, which represented 14.5 percent of the respondents, required employee contributions in addition to their own profit sharing contributions. This latter case was restricted to smaller firms which lacked finances to fund completely a company paid plan. Although less than one-half of the plants responded to the question regarding their motivations for changing their respective retirement programs, of those that did respond, 66 percent made changes in response to competitive pressure in the labor market, 29 percent made either inflation adjustments or minimized costs, and 10 percent made changes in response to legislative action. Again, however, it must be recalled that there are vesting periods associated with retirement programs (ten years) and due to the high

turnover nature of the industry, on average, most employees do not
vest, keeping costs down for the textile firms.

The last benefit explored in this study was time-off policy, including vacations, holidays, and personal leave. Table V-7 summarizes the results. Over 90 percent of the firms provide time-off
with pay in all three categories. The only significant variance appeared in the case of personal leave, where four firms permitted
personal leave without pay and three firms did not permit personal
leave.

Grievance Procedure

As might be expected, over 90 percent of the plants studied indicated the existence of a formal, documented, step-by-step grievance procedure. Three of the remaining eight plants employed a
procedure influenced by a union contract with the remainder lacking any formal procedure (see Table V-8).

TABLE V-8

Textile Industrial Relations
Grievance Procedure
28 Companies, 86 Plants

	Number	Percent
Formal	78	90.7
Informal	5	5.8
Union Contract	3	3.5

Source: Industrial Research Unit Textiles Questionnaire

With respect to the formal procedures, most involved a step-by-
step progression through management until the issue was satisfac-
torily resolved or the executive office was reached. The personnel
function usually acted as a mediator, ensuring both adherence to
the procedures and an opportunity for both parties to present their
respective cases. Furthermore, the personnel function usually provided a third party interpretation of the company's policies which
the grievance addressed.

In actual execution, informal grievance procedures did not differ
significantly from formal procedures. A similar step-by-step progression existed beginning with the employee's immediate super-
visor. In the informal case, however, an employee was not bound
by a documented procedure to follow a particular progression. Indeed, in every case the informal grievance procedure was identified
as an "open door policy" wherein an employee could take a grievance to any member of management at any time. On the surface,

this type of policy might appear preferable since an employee could bypass an individual he or she feels particularly uncomfortable in addressing. In actual practice, this may be detrimental to the employee's relationship with the individual skipped. Each manager should have the opportunity to confront and correct problems occurring within his sphere of responsibility without unfair recognition by the manager's supervisors or peers. It is in fairness to management that a step-by-step procedure is followed. It is in fairness to the employee that the personnel function mediates grievances.

SAFETY AND HEALTH

Although safety and health have long been issues in the textile industry, they have received increasing attention in recent years. As indicated in Chapter II, the emphasis in the industry has been on developing, implementing, and enforcing noise and dust standards. In response to employee needs and legislative action, the industry has taken many positive steps to ensure the health and safety of its employees in the workplace. Two of these steps are identified below.

One of the consistent steps taken in accordance with preventative and investigative concerns has been the formation of safety committees. The charter of these committees has been to conduct inspections, investigate accidents, and develop and implement safety awareness programs. Interestingly, the focus of the charter is on prevention. Even accident investigation is conducted with a goal of identifying measures for preventing a repeat accident. It is the safety awareness programs which are credited with reducing accidents to insignificant levels. Safety consciousness is stressed in training, reaffirmed in departmental meetings, posted throughout the plants, and often rewarded. In one case, a company picnic (at company expense) was given for an outstanding safety record. And the records have been outstanding. It is not unusual for a plant to operate up to a million person hours without any lost time because of an accident.

Although the charter of the safety committees has been consistent across companies, the makeup of these committees has been varied. In some cases the committee consists exclusively of management and, in others, a committee may have a mixture of management and blue-collar employees. Intuitively, it would be expected that the latter would be more successful. Peer pressure can provide effective motivation for maintaining safe working practices. Indeed, with the advent of participative management and quality circles, safety and health issues have been equally addressed by these employee groups alongside productivity and quality issues.

A second step taken by many firms, particularly the larger ones, has been the designation of a Corporate Safety and Health Department. This department provides technical assistance to the safety committees through environmental monitoring, designing and teaching safety courses, and acting upon committee recommendations. This action could come in the form of awareness of or actual correction of a hazard.

Preventive measures have also been taken in regard to worker health. Companies are using pre-employment medical evaluations and on-going health monitoring programs, and the industry believes that this practice is minimizing the threat of byssinosis.

Safety and health have been issues in the textile industry for some time and they will continue to be major issues in the future. This attention by employees, management, and government has resulted in significantly improved records in the immediate past. It is likely that additional improvements will be made as the industry modernizes. Newer plants and equipment are designed with an emphasis on health and safety, quality, and productivity. The three areas need not be mutually exclusive.

SUMMARY

This chapter has presented the results of a recent study on current personnel policies and practices in the industry. As shown, the industry is still populated with many smaller firms where personnel organizations are small and often not as professional as is warranted by the nature of the function. As a result, these smaller organizations are vulnerable to inconsistent practice. This is not to suggest that inconsistency is widespread, only that these firms often lack the well-developed policies and structure for implementing and executing policies to ensure consistent application.

On the other hand, the larger firms in the industry are much more sophisticated in policy development and practice. Surprisingly, however, much of the policy formulation remains under heavy influence of labor law firms which often also actively participate in the supervision and implementation of policy. The primary objectives here appear to be union avoidance in the years ahead.

With respect to the policies themselves, the industry has made tremendous strides in manpower concerns, scheduling and productivity, wages and benefits, and safety and health. Competition is forcing the industry to respond quickly and positively. Much of this competition is not foreign, nor even found within the industry; it is arising from other industries advancing to the Southeast. These other industries are competing with textiles for labor. This issue will continue as the general population ages and the number of young people in the workforce in the United States declines.

CHAPTER VI

Conclusion

The textile industry is labor intensive, geographically focused in about fifteen counties in North Carolina, South Carolina and Georgia, and dominated by the presence of small firms. In the most recent past, the industry has been moving toward modernization and centralization under pressures of declining labor availability, increasing imports, and government regulation. Women and minorities now play an important role in the unskilled and semi-skilled components of the textile labor force, and their presence is also being noted in white-collar areas. Change is inevitable in the industry and it appears from this study that the future will witness further consolidations and mergers resulting in larger firms. Prospects for a limited supply of labor will force companies to invest more of their resources in capital equipment and automation. While textile employment will continue to offer major opportunities for labor in the South, the absolute number of people employed will decrease in the future.

THE SOUTHERN INDUSTRIAL ENVIRONMENT

The textile industry once dominated employment in many southern communities; however, it is now being challenged as a leading employer by high technology industries such as metals, machinery, electrical, chemicals, and rubber. This industrial realignment is evident in some of the counties presented in this study, although some counties demonstrate more a potential for realignment than a mature diversification. A surprisingly large number of textile facilities are still located in places where they continue to be somewhat isolated from the mainstream of industrial development in the states and counties studied. This could change quickly over the next decade if consolidations and mergers continue in the textile industry. Plant closures and cutbacks in employment could lead to a recruitment of new industrial activity in the previously textile-dominant locations. The potential for an actualization of this realignment has prompted labor intensive industries, such as textiles, to respond with at least better wages and/or automation.

113

UNIONIZATION

Employers in the textile industry remain firmly committed to a union-free environment. The unions have failed to penetrate the United States textile industry, particularly in the South, during most of its long history. The failure on the part of the unions in recent years may have resulted from union weakness; however, management sophistication and expertise in aggressively responding to union advances may have played a major role in deterring union victories. The comprehensive communication programs, compensation and benefit upgrades, and consistency in policy formulation and application may have contributed substantially to the defeat of the unions. The unions have also concentrated much of their resources on the larger units in the textile industry and it appears that many of the small firms are still quite vulnerable to organization since they may not have the sophistication of larger firms in developing and administering personnel policies.

EMPLOYMENT POLICIES AND PRACTICES

As noted above, the textile industry is populated with many small firms where personnel organizations are relatively undeveloped and often not as professional as is warranted by the nature of the function. As a result, the smaller organizations are vulnerable to inconsistent practice. Inconsistency does not appear to be widespread, but the smaller firms appear to lack well-developed policies and structure for implementing and executing policies to ensure consistent application. The larger firms in the industry are much more sophisticated in their policy development and practice. It is surprising, however, that a great deal of the policy formulation in the industry remains under heavy influence of labor law firms which often also actively participate in the supervision and implementation of policy. Union avoidance seems to be a primary objective of the policy. Considerable progress seems to have been made in the industry in terms of developing practices pertaining to scheduling and productivity, wages and benefits, and safety and health. Competition has forced the industry to respond in an effective manner. Industrial activity in the Sunbelt and the Southeast have provided a great deal of competition and motivation for the textile industry to review their practices. The industries moving into the textile areas are competing with textiles for labor. This is an issue that will continue as the population ages and the number of young people in the workforce declines.

THE FUTURE

The textile industry will continue to be a major employer in parts of the South, but the composition of the labor force will continue to change. Women and minorities will likely play an increasingly significant role in both blue-collar and white-collar occupations in the industry. The total number of employees will continue to decline as a result of automation, new technology, consolidations, and mergers.

It appears that the industry will be in a position to reap the benefits of large investments in capital equipment in the future. Productivity increases should be sizable as a large number of people is eliminated and new equipment is substituted.

The import problem will remain with the industry and trade associations, such as the American Textile Manufacturer's Institute, will have to remain vigilant in protecting the interests of American manufacturers. This necessary activity for the long term viability of the industry will divert resources that could be used in other constructive ways, including activities involving human resources management.

Personnel policies and programs that have been developed recently should continue to make a positive contribution to human resources management in the future. Physical facilities have been improved dramatically in many textile areas and employee needs have been given a great deal of attention by progressive textile employers. The modern textile plant is clean, air conditioned, less noisy, dust free, and generally a pleasant place to work. The unions are not likely to make much additional headway in these environments. A combination of factors is likely to frustrate the union's efforts to organize employees in the textile industry, including a lessened need for outside representation of employee interests as employers develop positive personnel policies and programs. Employees have begun to turn more to government and to lawyers to protect their interests, and the unions appear to have limited resources and less of a commitment to organize. In some instances, of course, the absence of the union has had little to do with the effectiveness of management but it is a reflection of ineffectiveness on the part of the labor movement. Recently, however, the Amalgamated Clothing and Textile Workers Union announced a victory—"the largest union victory in the Carolinas in years" [1]—in an organizing drive against Reeves Brothers in North Carolina, re-

[1] AFL-CIO, Industrial Union Department, *Labor & Investments,* Vol. 6, No. 3 (April 1986), pp. 1 and 8.

sulting in the organization of 750 people. This victory is attributed to a corporate campaign wherein the union was able to involve aspects of the pension investment program to their advantage. Time will tell whether or not this particular approach will be successfully implemented by the union in the future.

The merger and consolidation movement in the textile industry, which has received a great deal of momentum in the past few years, is likely to continue resulting in larger firms. It will become increasingly difficult for the small firms to survive, and this may result in a much different industry than we have witnessed in the past. When these developments occur, it will be necessary for management to invest in more professional human resources management, and this should lead to a better utilization of the industrial relations practitioner and, consequently, to a declining and different role for the outside legal advisor.

APPENDIX

Textile Study Questionnaire

1. Company:
   Name: _____
   Location: _____
   _____ (County)

2. What is the structure of the industrial relations/personnel function in the company?
   Title of senior industrial relations/personnel manager?
   _____

   To whom does the industrial relations/personnel manager report?
   _____

   What are the chief responsibilities of the industrial relations/personnel manager?
   _____
   _____

   Please specify job titles and describe duties of others employed in the industrial relations/personnel function:
   _____
   _____
   _____

2. (a) In the case of the multi-plant company, is the industrial relations/personnel policy coordinated at company headquarters level? Yes ____ No ____
   To what extent is there a centralized corporate-wide personnel policy?
   _____

3. Total Employment: _____
   Number of hourly production and maintenance workers: ____
   Number of other employees (managerial employees): _____

4. Are employees represented by a union? Yes ____ No ____
   If "yes," give name of union: _____
   Date union was certified: _____
   Have there been any recent organizing activities at the plant?
   Yes ____ No ____
   If there have been organizing activities, indicate which union and nature of the activities: _____
   _____

APPENDIX *(continued)*

5. What is the turnover rate for production and maintenance workers?

    Has the rate risen over the past decade? Yes ____ No ____
    If "yes," to what do you attribute the rise? _____

    _____

    Is there any evidence that new industry moving into the area/county has caused employees to leave the company? Yes ____ No ____
    Explain briefly: _____

    _____

    _____

6. What proportion of workers would you estimate are hired as a result of the following:

    referrals by employees _____
    referrals by relatives _____
    walk-ins _____
    college/high school recruiting _____
    newspaper ads _____
    TV/radio ads _____
    employment agencies _____

7. What minimum qualifications, if any, are required for employment?

    _____

8. What type of training period is provided for entry-level jobs? Please specify length of training period and who provides the training.

    _____

    _____

    _____

9. Is there an initial probationary period required for production and maintenance personnel? Yes ____ No ____

    If "yes," how long is the period? _____
    Is there a wage differential associated with the probationary period?
    Yes ____ No ____
    If "yes," please state differential _____

10. What is the company policy regarding promotion? _____

    _____

    _____

    Please indicate if the firm generally promotes from within and if there is a bidding procedure for new openings: _____

    _____

APPENDIX *(continued)*

11. What were the average weekly hours for production and maintenance employees for 1980? _____

12. What is the estimated number of hours lost for the average employee because of unpaid, unauthorized absenteeism or tardiness in 1980? _____

13. Is overtime a usual occurrence in the plant? Yes ____ No ____
    What is the average overtime hours worked?
    (a) at 1 1/2 time _____
    (b) at double time _____

14. Does the company operate on a continuous shift basis? (24 hours, 7 days / week). Yes ____ No ____
    If "yes," please state number of employees on continuous shift in 1980. _____
    What was the length of shifts? _____

15. Does the company operate on a noncontinuous shift basis? Yes ____ No ____
    If "yes," please state number of employees on continuous shift operations in 1980 _____
    What was the length of shifts? _____

16. What type of shift was most often scheduled in 1980?
    (a) 1 shift—4 days _____
    (b) 1 shift—5 days _____
    (c) 2 shifts—5 days _____
    (d) 2 shifts—6 days _____
    (e) 2 shifts—7 days _____
    (f) 3 shifts—5 days _____
    (g) 3 shifts—6 days _____
    (h) 3 shifts—7 days _____
    (i) Other, please specify _____

17. Are shifts fixed or rotating? _____

18. How many employees work part-time? _____
    Has the number of part-time workers increased in the past decade?
    Yes ____ No ____

19. How are wage increases determined in your plant?
    _____
    _____

20. To what extent are wage increases influenced by:
    (a) industry-wide developments? _____
    (b) an industry leader? _____
    (c) local wage developments? _____

APPENDIX *(continued)*

21. Has there been pressure for wage increases because of recent expansion of new firms in the area/county? Yes ____ No ____. Please explain briefly.

_____
_____

22. How do wages in your plant compare to those of other firms in your locality?

_____

23. If employees are organized, what impact does the union have on wage increases?

_____
_____

    Do unionized employees receive higher wage increases than non-unionized employees? _____

24. Is there a cost of living (COLA) provision in effect in your plant? Yes ____ No ____
    If "yes," when was this instituted and under what formula? _

_____

25. What is the policy in regard to shift differentials in the plant?

_____
_____
_____
_____
_____

26. What is the policy in regard to the following benefits involving payment for time not worked?
    (a) Vacation days: _____
    (b) Holidays: _____
    (c) Maternity leave: _____
    (d) Breaks from work: _____

27. What is the policy in regard to insurance protection; does the company provide any of the following:
    (a) medical insurance? _____
    (b) life insurance? _____

28. Does the company provide pension benefits? Yes ____ No ____
    If "yes," please indicate the level of benefits: _____

_____

29. Have revisions been made in benefit schedules over the past 5 years?
    Yes ____ No ____
    If "yes," what has caused the revisions? _____

_____

APPENDIX *(continued)*

30. What is the procedure in the plant for handling employee grievances?

_____

_____

31. If there is a formal procedure for handling grievances, please indicate the steps taken to resolve the grievance.

_____

_____

32. Please indicate how much of an impact you think industrial development in the South, and particularly in your locality, has influenced decisions that have been made in the personnel/ employee relations area in the past decade.

_____

_____

33. To what extent has your specific company's personnel/industrial relations policies changed in regard to the impact discussed in the above question (32)?

_____

_____

_____

34. What impact do you think new technology and capital investment will have on the size and character of the labor force in the future?

_____

_____

_____

35. Do you think that there will be significant (major) changes in the way that the company handles employee relations in the ensuing 10 years?
Yes _____ No _____
If "yes," why do you think the changes will be made? _____

36. Occupational health and safety have been matters of concern to the textile industry. Would you answer the following questions in regard to these matters:
(A) Would you kindly describe the basic features of the plant's safety program?

_____

_____

_____

_____

_____

(B) What positive results have you seen from the program in the past year?

_____

_____

_____

37. Would you indicate to us any aspect of the questionnaire that you think is inadequate in terms of leading to a clear under-standing of the way in which employee relations are handled in the textile industry?

_____

_____

_____

_____

_____

Index